CISTERCIAN FATHERS SERI

CW00516793

## BERNARD OF CLAIRVAUX

# IN PRAISE OF THE NEW KNIGHTHOOD

CISTERCIAN FATHERS SERIES: NUMBER NINETEEN B

# IN PRAISE OF THE NEW KNIGHTHOOD

## A TREATISE ON THE KNIGHTS TEMPLAR AND THE HOLY PLACES OF JERUSALEM

by
**BERNARD OF CLAIRVAUX**

Translated by M. Conrad Greenia ocso

Introduction by Malcolm Barber

Cistercian Publications

A Cistercian Publications title published by Liturgical Press

**Cistercian Publications**
Editorial Offices
Abbey of Gethsemani
3642 Monks Road
Trappist, Kentucky 40051
www.cistercianpublications.org

A translation of *In laude novae militiae* from the critical latin edition
prepared by Jean Leclercq OSB and H. M. Rochais under the sponsorship of
the Order of Cistercians and published in *Sancti Bernardi Opera*, vol. 3.
Rome: Editiones Cistercienses, 1963.

The work of Cistercian Publications is made possible in part
by support from Western Michigan University to
The Institute of Cistercian Studies

# TABLE OF CONTENTS

# TABLE OF ABBREVIATIONS

Asspt       Sermon for the Assumption

BSJ         Bruno Scott James, translator.
            *The Letters of Saint Bernard of Clairvaux.* London:
            Burns & Oates, 1953; rpt. London: Sutton-Kalamazoo:
            Cistercian Publications, 1998.

Ep[p]       *Epistola(e)*; Letter(s)

LXX         Septuagint

PL          *Patrologia latina cursus completus, series latina.*
            221 volumes. Edited J.-P. Migne. Paris, 1844-1864.

RB          *Saint Benedict's Rule for Monasteries.* The critical edi-
            tion is *RB1980.* Edited by Timothy Fry, Imogene Baker,
            Timothy Horner, Augustine Raabe, Mark Sheridan.
            Collegeville: Liturgical Press, 1980.
            Citations are made by chapter and verse.

SBOp        *Sancti Bernardi Opera*, 8 volumes. Edited Jean Leclercq,
            H. M. Rochais, C. H. Talbot.
            Rome: Editiones Cistercienses, 1957-1977.

Vita Bern   *Sancti Bernardi Abbatis Clarae-vallensis Vita et Res Gestae.*
            PL 185:225-368.

# INTRODUCTION

'**O**WHAT GREAT DIFFERENCES and dissimilarities of all kinds there are between contemplation and meditation among the pillars of the cloister and the terrible exercise of warfare!'[1] Thus wrote Richard de Templo, prior of the augustinian house of the Holy Trinity in London, as he described the ferocity of the battle between the crusaders and the forces of Saladin at Arsuf in September 1191. Richard seems to have compiled his account largely for a monastic audience, and he evidently expected that this audience would readily recognise the stark contrast between these two ways of life. Yet he was probably writing sometime between 1217 and 1222, approximately a century after the formation of the Order of the Temple. During the intervening years the concept of a monastic order whose members fought terrestrial wars on Christ's behalf had apparently been fully absorbed into contemporary life. In the decade that followed the papal recognition of the Temple at the Council of Troyes in January 1129, the Hospitallers added military functions to their charitable activities, while between 1164 and 1176 the Spanish military orders of Calatrava, Alcántara, and Santiago, were created. The Teutonic Knights, who were to become as important as their Templar and Hospitaller predecessors, were also well-established by the 1220s, having developed from a german field hospital during these same campaigns and in 1198 received a Rule based on that of the Templars. If, therefore, the polarisation between monk and warrior remained acute even in the second decade of the thirteenth century, it can be seen that, when Bernard of Clairvaux wrote his treatise *In Praise of the New Knighthood* sometime around 1130, he was indeed entering new territory—which fully justified his statement that his subject was that of 'a new kind of knighthood and one unknown to the ages gone by'.

---

[1] *Itinerarium Peregrinum et Gesta Regis Ricardi*, ed. W. Stubbs, *Chronicles and Memorials of the Reign of Richard I*, vol. 1, Rolls Series 38 (London, 1864) p. 270.

To understand the nature of the treatise therefore it is necessary to examine the circumstances of its composition. According to the Prologue, Bernard had been asked three times to offer in writing moral support to the Templars, support which would be far more valuable than any material aid he could give. The 'dear Hugh' who made the requests is Hugh of Payns who, together with Godfrey of Saint Omer, and a group of knights at that time living in the Kingdom of Jerusalem, seems to have asked the patriarch in the course of the year 1119, if they could serve the charitable function of giving succour and protection to pilgrims travelling from the port of Jaffa to Jerusalem and to the holy places in its vicinity. It was probably on the occasion of the reforming council of Nablus of January 1120, that they took vows before the patriarch to dedicate themselves to this work to the exclusion of all else. King Baldwin II, Patriarch Warmund of Picquigny, and the canons of the Temple of the Lord, who occupied the Dome of the Rock in Jerusalem, provided clothing and equipment, together with accommodation in the Temple area. When, sometime in the 1120s, the king moved his base from the al-Aqsa mosque—which the crusaders called the Temple of Solomon—to the Tower of David on the west side of the city, the way was clear for Hugh and his followers to take over the southern part of the Templar platform, which thereafter became their headquarters.[2]

At this stage, the anomaly of a warrior-monk was not at all evident to a society in which prominent ecclesiastics increasingly assigned members of that society to their own defined *ordo*. It seems likely that the knights had originally conceived of their role as a kind of lay fraternity, perhaps associated with the Hospitallers who had been providing food and shelter for visiting pilgrims since well before the arrival of the first crusaders and who had already been given official recognition by the Church in 1113. Indeed, it has been speculated that the 'proto-Templars' had actually lived in the Hospital adjacent to the Holy Sepulchre and that

---

2    See M. Barber, *The New Knighthood. A History of the Order of the Templ*
(Cambridge, 1994) pp. 3-11.

they had been dependent upon the canons, a situation which might explain the augustinian elements in their first Rule of 1129.[3] Directing the energies of Hugh and his knights towards actual physical protection of travellers therefore neatly complemented the Hospitaller function in an environment in which inadequate Christian forces were already stretched too far to fulfil all the duties required of them. Professing monastic vows did not make them monks; it simply underlined their commitment to a pious cause, while laying up potential credit towards their own personal salvation.

The acquisition of a written latin Rule of seventy-two clauses from the fathers at the Council of Troyes in January 1129, fundamentally altered this informal arrangement. 'So I exhort you', says the Prologue of the Rule, 'who up until now have embraced a secular knighthood in favour of humans only, and in which Christ was not the cause, to hasten to associate yourself in perpetuity with the order of those whom God has chosen from the mass of perdition and has assembled for the defence of the Holy Church'.[4] This Rule was based in part on an oral presentation Hugh of Payns made before the council. He had travelled to the West in 1127 on a double mission: to help recruit soldiers for a new campaign against Damascus; and to present the case for recognition. Bernard of Clairvaux, to whom Hugh was related, attended the council and this may have been one of the occasions when Hugh attempted to persuade him to write a treatise in support of the nascent Order. He may have felt in need of the help of his increasingly prestigious relative; a letter of a person calling himself 'Hugh the Sinner', which probably dates from about this time, suggests that doubts had been cast upon the validity of this new profession. The writer of the letter is not known, although the mediocre quality of the Latin and the inaccuracy of the biblical citations make it more likely to be the work of a pious layman such as Hugh of Payns himself than that of a high-powered intel-

---

3   See A. Luttrell, 'The Earliest Templars', in *Autour de la Prèmière Croisade*, ed. M. Balard (Paris, 1996) pp. 193-202.

4   *La Régle du Temple*, ed. H. de Curzon, Société de l'Histoire de France (Paris, 1886) p. 12.

lectual such as Hugh of Saint Victor, both of whom have been
cited as possible authors.[5] In any event the letter makes clear that
some (unnamed) persons had challenged the validity of the
Templars' occupation and that that challenge had been suffi-
ciently forceful to cause the early Templars themselves to have
their own doubts. 'Hugh the Sinner' assures the brothers that
everybody has a proper function for 'each receives his recom-
pense according to his work'. He explains that he is telling them
this because he knows that their minds have been troubled by
persons who are so foolish as to suggest that lives consecrated to
the defence of Christians menaced by the enemies of faith and
peace might, in some way, be directed towards an illicit or sinful
goal. Such accusations he calls tares sown by the devil, who 'is
always trying and working cruelly to bring about the corruption
of good work'.[6]

Neither the letter of 'Hugh the Sinner' nor Saint Bernard's *In
Praise of the New Knighthood* can be securely dated, nor is it
known whether either or both were written before or after the
promulgation of the Rule in January 1129. As *In Praise of the
New Knighthood* is addressed to Hugh of Payns scholars have usually assumed that it was written before his death, which cannot
have been later than 24 May 1137, but which may have been as
early as 1134.[7] It seems unlikely to have preceded the letter of
'Hugh the Sinner', which would surely have been redundant in
the light of a major treatise by the leading Cistercian of his day.
The letter itself was probably written in the West to the small
group of Templars still in the East. If it really is the work of Hugh
of Payns, then it is most likely that he wrote it during his exten-

---

5    See J. Leclercq, 'Un document sur les débuts des Templiers', *Revue d'histoire
     ecclésiastique*, 52 (1957) 81-91, which includes the latin text, and
     C. Sclafert, 'Lettre inédite de Hugues de Saint-Victor aux Chevaliers du
     Temple', *Revue d'ascétique et de mystique*, 34 (1958) 276-299. The most re-
     cent discussion is by D. Selwood, '*Quidam autem dubitaverunt*: The Saint and
     the Sinner, the Temple and a Possible Chronology', in *Autour de la Pre-
     mière Croisade* (above, n.3) pp. 223-4, who favours Hugh of Payns as
     the author.
6    Leclercq, 'Un document', 86-87.
7    See Barber, p. 342, n.123.

sive absence in France, England, and Scotland between 1127 and
1129. There is little internal evidence for dating *In Praise of the
New Knighthood*, although Saint Bernard's major preoccupation
with the sins of secular knights accords closely with the contrast
drawn in the Prologue to the Rule between the profession of the
Templars which is 'worthy, holy and sublime' and those who 'do
not strive to protect the poor in the churches, which was their
duty, but rather rob, despoil, and kill'.[8] Bernard's presence at
Troyes makes it inconceivable that he did not have considerable
influence upon the Rule, even if it is now thought unlikely that
he actually drafted it.[9] Unfortunately, it is not possible to be certain which document came first, despite the similarities. A likely chronology might be: the letter of 'Hugh the Sinner' (1128),
the latin Rule (1129), *In Praise of the New Knighthood* (1130).[10]
Nevertheless, the problems of dating and chronology remain.

Bernard begins by making a distinction between two kinds of
warfare: the spiritual, characteristic of monks and fought against

---

8   *Règle*, p. 12.

9   Recent scholarship has tended to emphasise the augustinian aspects of the
    Rule. See Luttrell, p.201, and M.-L. Bulst-Thiele, 'The Influence of St Bernard
    of Clairvaux on the Formation of the Knights Templar', in *The Second Crusade
    and the Cistercians*, ed. M. Gervers (New York, 1992) pp. 59-60.

10  For speculations about this chronology, see D. Carlson, 'The Practical Theology
    of St Bernard and the date of the *De Laude novae militiae*', in *Erudition at
    God's Service*, ed. J. R. Sommerfeldt, Studies in Medieval Cistercian History, 11
    (Kalamazoo, 1997) pp. 142-145, who thinks that 'In Praise of the New Knight-
    hood' was written after the Council of Troyes, but before November 1130, when
    Innocent II issued his prohibition on tournaments at the Council of Clermont.
    He argues that if it had been written after the tournament ban, Saint Bernard
    would have mentioned this.
    Selwood, '*Quidam autem dubitaverunt*', pp. 226-269, also attempts to date the
    treatise on the basis of what it does not contain rather than what it does. He argues
    that it shows no knowledge of what occurred at Troyes, nor of the quite rapid
    expansion of the 1130s, and therefore it predates the council. For him, Troyes
    marks the culmination of these events, for the Templars would have had no
    need of the exhortations contained in the letter of 'Hugh the Sinner', or in St
    Bernard's treatise, after they had received this official recognition. This is a
    plausible theory, but in the end it is a speculation resting upon a speculation.
    P.-Y. Emery thinks that it must be dated nearer to the mid-1130s on the basis
    that the content of the treatise implies that the Templars already had a certain
    renown: Bernard of Clairvaux, *Oeuvres complètes*, vol. 31. *Eloge de la Nouvelle*

the invisible forces of evil; and the physical, undertaken by knights against terrestrial and material enemies. Neither are remarkable, he says, as both are common. The Templars, however, are involved in a form of battle 'hitherto unknown' in that they fight in both ways, a role which gives them a double armour and means they need fear neither life nor death. Drawing both on the monastic interpreters of the First Crusade, who wrote in the years immediately following the fall of Jerusalem in 1099, and on the powerful self-image of the first crusaders, he presents these men as holy martyrs.[11] Directly opposed to them is the 'worldly warrior' who, in contrast to the double protection of the Templar, runs a double risk: if he dies himself he suffers physical death; while if he kills another he dies a spiritual death. The key is motivation, or in augustinian terms, right intention. Pride, revenge, or even self-defence, are unjustifiable reasons for killing; only when the motive is pure can fighting not be considered evil.

While ultimately these arguments as rooted in Saint Augustine's definition of just war—that is, one fought on proper authority, with right intention, and for a just cause[12]—nevertheless their immediate context can be found in the calling of the First Crusade by Pope Urban II in 1095, and in the success of those

---

*Chevalerie. Vie de Saint Malachie*, introd., trans., notes et index par P.-Y. Emery (Paris, 1990) p. 21. See, too, the discussions in F. Cardini, *I Poveri Cavalieri del Cristo. Bernardo di Clairvaux e la Fondazione dell'Ordine Templare* (Rimini, 1992) pp.89, 100, 120, and J. Fleckenstein, 'Die Rechtfertigung der geistlichen Ritterorden nach der Schrift "De laude novae militiae" Bernhards von Clairvaux', in *Die geistlichen Ritterorden Europas*, ed. J. Fleckenstein and M. Hellmann (Sigmaringen, 1980) pp.9-11. It should also be noted how incredibly busy Saint Bernard was during the decade 1125 to 1135, a period which saw the flourishing of his literary activity, beginning with *De gradibus humilitatis et superbiae*, the *Apologia* to William of Saint Thierry, and his early letters and sermons, continuing with *De gratia et libero arbitrio* and *De dilgendo Deo*, and culminating in the *Semones super Cantica Canticorum*, as well as his frequent public activities. It is not surprising that he found it necessary to make excuses for his tardiness in actually writing *De Laude*, which must be viewed as one of his lesser literary works.

11  For the context, see H.E.J. Cowdrey, 'Martyrdom and the First Crusade', in *Crusade and Settlement*, ed. P. W. Edbury (Cardiff, 1985) pp. 46-56.

12  See F. H. Russell, *The Just War in the Middle Ages* (Cambridge, 1975) pp. 16-39.

who responded in capturing the city of Jerusalem in 1099.[13] Urban's ideas had, in turn, their genesis among the reformers assembled at the papal court in the second half of the eleventh century, particularly those around Gregory VII (1073-1085), the most militant of the reform popes of the period. The most important of these reformers was Anselm, bishop of Lucca, who between 1083 and 1086 formulated a coherent and authoritative guide to the circumstances in which it was permissible for a Christian to wage war.[14] Within a decade, three french monastic writers—Guibert of Nogent, Robert the Monk, and Baudric of Bourgeuil—had—apparently unknown to each other—presented the victory of the First Crusade as a manifest sign of God's approval and portrayed its participants as christian soldiers who could obtain salvation through legitimate warfare. Although none of them had been participants, they moulded the ideas and feelings of those who had been into a structured presentation of ethical knighthood. In the past, salvation had been almost exclusively reserved for monks, but by God's miracle, a different path to heaven was now offered to the secular knight, even though before the crusade he might have been motivated entirely by savagery and greed.[15] In the view of Colin Morris, the turn of the century was a crucial period of new thinking about knighthood, one in which clerical writers, quite consciously innovating, made

---

13  The extent to which Saint Bernard was picking up these papal themes in the first part of the treatise can be seen by comparing the sources for the pope's speech (both the chronicles and the letters) with 'In Praise of the New Knighthood'. For the chronicle sources, see D. C. Munro, 'The Speech of Pope Urban II at Clermont', *American Historical Review*, 11 (1906) 231-242. See, too, J. Richard, *The Crusades*, c.1071- c.1291, tr. J. Birrell (Cambridge, 1999) pp. 19-27, in particular his explanation of the appeal of Urban's words to the warrior classes.

14  See J. Leclercq, 'St Bernard's Attitude toward War', in *Studies in Medieval Cistercian History*, 2, ed. J.R. Sommerfeldt (Kalamazoo, 1976) pp. 8-10, 31.

15  See J. Riley-Smith, *The First Crusade and the Idea of Crusading* (Philadelphia, 1986) pp. 135-152, with copious quotation from these three writers; C. J. Holdsworth, 'Ideas and Reality: Some Attempts to Control and Defuse War in the Twelfth Century', in *Studies in Church History*, 20 (1983), 59-78; and R. W. Kaeuper, *Chivalry and Violence in Medieval Europe* (Oxford, 1999) pp. 73-75.

a real attempt to define knighthood as a legitimate order.[16] Indeed, as Jonathan Riley-Smith sees it, monastic literature of first decade after 1099 presented the First Crusade almost in terms of a vast, mobile monastery, whose members practised common ownership, chastity, and frugality—an image which strikingly prefigures the Order of the Temple.[17] These works, written for a monastic audience by Benedictines with no direct experience of actual warfare, had resonances among the warrior class as well, for ever since the conversion of the germanic tribes they had fought their wars imbued with the conviction that God was on their side. The performance of religious rites in conjunction with their warlike lifestyle came quite naturally to them and indeed the Church's provision of appropriate 'mechanisms of atonement' became an integral part of this lifestyle.[18] Thus the establishment of an institutional form of monastic knighthood developed logically from contemporary clerical interpretations of the crusade, as well as fitting neatly into the value system of the knightly classes, and it is not surprising to find Saint Bernard drawing on the same themes in his efforts to justify this new order.

Thereafter, Bernard builds on these arguments by concentrating upon the evils of those contemporary warriors whose activities did not accord with the standards of an ethical knighthood. Here some historians have thought that the treatise was intended to reach a wider audience than simply the small number of men who had already committed themselves to the Temple.[19] Certainly his message seems to be aimed at secular knights, whose activities he tries to shame by presenting them as essentially

16   C. Morris, 'Equestris ordo: Chivalry as a Vocation in the Twelfth Century', in Studies in Church History, 15 (1978) pp. 87-88.

17   Riley-Smith, First Crusade and the Idea of Crusading, p. 150.

18   See M. Strickland, War and Chivalry, The Conduct and Perception of War in England and Normandy, 1066-1217 (Cambridge, 1996) pp. 55-57, 92.

19   Carlson, 'Practical Theology', p. 137, and Emery, p.19. J. Leclercq, Monks and Love in Twelfth-Century France (Oxford, 1979) p. 21, sees the treatise more as an expression of Saint Bernard's 'own ideal of knighthood' than as a way 'to propagate interest in a nascent institution'.

effeminate. Members of the 'worldly knighthood, or rather knavery' ride out in long, flowing robes quite unsuitable for combat, their vainglorious appearance emphasised by the coloured trappings on their armour and horses. These he describes as 'the trinkets of a woman', just as he sees their long flowing hair as 'effeminate locks'. This image of the long-haired knight—vain, lascivious, and frivolous—was well-established. Contemporary artistic representation of women with long and unkempt hair was usually meant to represent wantonness,[20] a characteristic frequently attributed to secular knights by ecclesiastical writers. According to Serlo, bishop of Séez, who, at Carentan in Normandy at Easter 1105, castigated Henry I and his men for wearing long hair, it was shameful for men to be seen in this way, for long hair was enjoined on penitents as an outward sign of their inner sinfulness. Such hair was suitable only for women; it was quite inappropriate for those who ought to exhibit manly strength. As Orderic Vitalis, the chronicler of the norman house of Saint Evroult, describes the incident, his words had immediate effect: Henry and the nobles at once cut off their luxuriant tresses.[21] Again, therefore, Saint Bernard returns to the key question of motivation: secular knights are driven by anger, glory or greed. 'It is certainly not safe to kill or be killed for such causes as these.'

The concomitant of God's new path to salvation for secular knights, as presented by ecclesiastical writers, therefore, is that it is not acccessible to those who refuse to adhere to the Church's standards. This was not an entirely disinterested position, for monasteries and churches were often the victims of knightly aggression and, as early as the late tenth century, attempts had

---

20  See R. M. Wright, 'The Great Whore in the Illustrated Apocalypse Cycles', *Journal of Medieval History*, 23 (1997) 199.

21  *The Ecclesiastical History of Orderic Vitalis*, ed. and trans. M. Chibnall (Oxford, 1978) vol. 6: pp. 64-67, and notes 1-4. Saint Anselm, at that time archbishop of Canterbury, had already condemned long hair in men for similar reasons. Serlo alleged that such men were fornicators and sodomites: 'The perverse sons of Belial grow the tresses of women on their heads and deck their toes with the tails of scorpions, revealing themselves to be effeminate by their softness and serpent-like by their scorpion stings.'

been made, first to impose the peace of God, which tried to protect certain vulnerable social groups in time of war, and then,
from the 1020s, the truce of God, aimed at prohibiting warfare
at certain periods of the year such as Easter or days of the week
such as Sunday.[22] These measures do not seem to have had much
practical effect. Matthew Strickland, for example, shows that
such restrictions showed little or no appreciation of the exigencies
of warfare, which often precluded the temporary cessation of hos-
tilities or fine distinctions between legitimate and illegitimate tar-
gets. In this sense the monastic writers tried to have their cake
and eat it, for they sought both protection and donations from
their local aristocracy who, in turn, gained prestige from such
associations. Yet inevitably such close links with a particular
noble family made the monastery in question an obvious target
for the enemies of that family.[23] Nor were the ecclesiastical writers the only purveyors of standards, for the warrior class has its
own codes and objectives, which most of them regarded as perfectly legitimate. Warfare could bring glory and prestige–and,
indeed, even Saint Bernard admits that 'death in battle is more
precious as it is the more glorious'—while adherence to the con-
ventions on such matters as ransom and truces were essential (and
usually practical) elements in the building of reputation among
the aristocracy.[24]

Even so *In Praise of the New Knighthood* shows very clearly that
ecclesiastical writers had not given up. Far from it. They had
found in the crusading ethos a new lever to use against a recalci-
trant aristocracy. Bernard's diatribe was followed by those of other
distinguished twelfth-century writers, including Peter of Blois,
John of Salisbury, Stephen of Fougères, and Alain of Lille.[25] The

---

22   See H.E.J. Cowdrey, 'The Peace and Truce of God in the Eleventh Century',
     *Past and Present*, 46 (1970) pp. 42-67.

23   Strickland, pp. 90-91; E. Mason, '*Timeo Barones et Donas Ferentes*', in *Studies
     in Church History*, 15 (1978) pp. 61-62.

24   Strickland, p. 35.

25   See Kaeuper, pp. 77-80, and D. Carlson, 'Religious Writers and Church Coun-
     cils on Chivalry', in *The Study of Chivalry. Resources and Approaches*, ed. H.
     Chickering and T. H. Seiler (Kalamazoo, 1988) pp. 144-145.

formation and subsequent popularity of the military orders shows
that this was a more successful line of approach than that of the
peace movements, for both the Templars and Hospitallers became
wealthy corporations based upon vast networks of european preceptories, the foundations of which had been built from the
donations of this same warrior aristocracy. Moreover, many of
these men gave up their secular way of life and joined the orders,
not in their dotage or after age or injury precluded further material activities—as was so often the case with traditional benedic-
tine orders—but while they were in their prime, willing and able
to fight for what both they and Bernard saw as a just cause. The
perception of historians that aristocratic donations to monasteries were often niggardly, that they were 'gesture politics'[26] quite
subordinate to the fundamental need to protect the basic structure of the lordship, is not always borne out in analyses of donations to military orders. The Templar preceptory of Richerenches
in the Vaucluse, for example, which was established in the 1130s,
was largely based upon the patrimony of the Bourbouton family, whose male members themselves joined the Order and ran
the house, leaving little of the original lordship intact, except for
what was needed for their former dependents.[27]

Bernard's rhetoric on the negativity of the worldly *malitia* is followed by a positive appreciation of the true *militia*. If the condemnation of secular knights was written with an eye on this particular constituency, then this section shows an acute awareness of
clerical opinion as well. Once again, Bernard's approach suggests
that this treatise was intended to be much more than simply a pri-
vate communication to the Templars in the East, even if it is true
that he had been pushed into writing it by Hugh of Payns. In
Bernard's view Christianity is not a pacifist religion. There is no
prohibition on killing *per se*, as long as the right motive exists.
The fact that John the Baptist bid soldiers be content with their
pay shows it was possible for Christians 'to strike with the sword',
a view quite contrary to that of men like Peter Damian, who had

---

26  Mason, p. 61.
27  See Barber, pp. 260-261.

tried to counter the militant Christianity of the mid-eleventh century reform papacy.[28] While he was not arguing that pagans be slaughtered if they could be prevented from harming the faithful by other means, it was necessary to use force if these other means were not available or had failed. This is clearly disingenuous. Bernard himself came from a knightly background and must have been well-aware that the average crusader was hardly likely to pose this question to himself before wading into battle. Nor, indeed, is there any evidence of extensive diplomatic activity among the Muslim powers by Urban II before he launched an expedition which he liked to present in defensive terms. As the crusaders saw it, the crusade was an expedition to recover the holy places from pagans who, in the words of Robert the Monk, had unjustly invaded 'our lands'.[29] Again, the First Crusade provides the context for Bernard's remarks.

The Templar virtues are reflected in their lifestyle, which Bernard undertakes to set out 'briefly'. Not surprisingly, in several ways, he sounds as if he is describing the Cistercians. Austerity and moderation are the keys, for the Templars are obedient, plain in dress and habits, chaste, and communal. They avoid excess in food and clothing, in contrast to secular knights, just as members of monastic orders should refrain from the elaborate building programmes of some of their contemporaries—a point already made very explicitly by Saint Bernard in his *Apologia* to William of Saint Thierry, written shortly before in the mid-1120s.[30] More specifically, they keep themselves occupied in rare moments when they are not on duty by repairing their equipment, and they avoid contemporary frivolities such as dice, chess, hunting, falconry,

28   See Leclercq, 'St Bernard's Attitude Toward War', pp. 22-27.

29   Robert the Monk, *Historia Iherosolimitana*, in *Receuil des Historiens des Croisades. Historiens Occidentaux*, vol. 3 (Paris, 1866) p. 792.

30   Bernard of Clairvaux, 'Apologia ad Guillelmum Abbatem', in *S. Bernardii Opera*, vol. 3: *Tractatus et opuscula*, ed. J. Leclercq and H. Rochais (Rome, 1963), caps. IX, pp.20-1, X, pp. 24-26, XII, 28-29. On this issue see C. Rudolph, *The 'Things of Greater Importance': Bernard of Clairvaux's Apologia and the Medieval Attitude towards Art* (Philadelphia, 1990) esp. pp. 159-191.

jesters, troubadours, and jousts. They do not waste time in idle conversation or laughter. Merit and not their former social class determine their reputations.[31] As a summary of the leisure-time pursuits of the secular knighthood, these observations add new emphasis to Bernard's contrast between the two kinds of warrior. The reference to tournaments is particularly pertinent, for Pope Innocent II (of whom Saint Bernard was a strong supporter) had begun what proved to be a long series of prohibitions at the Council of Clermont in 1130. His restriction was repeated six times between then and the Fourth Lateran Council of 1215, evidence both of its ineffectiveness and of the strength of ecclesiastical opposition to this aspect of the knightly life-style.[32] Bernard's disgust at the participation of knights in a tournament almost immediately after they had returned from the Second Crusade (1147-8) reflects his continued belief in the distinction between knights who maintained proper ethical conduct and those distracted by the superficialities of the material world.[33]

Most important of all is the Templar conduct in battle. There their sober and quiet approach contrasts with the gaudy ornamentation of the secular knighthood. They do not calculate the odds, for they know that God is on their side and are convinced, like the Maccabees, that victory is therefore certain. That they cut their hair and care nothing for washing shows their complete indifference to the bodily vanities of secular knights. Here the Templars accord with the idealised portrait of the knights of the First Crusade as described by Robert the Monk. These men 'do not fear death or the enemy... When they prepare for battle they raise their lances high and then advance in ranks, as silently as though they were dumb.'[34] The Templars are the actual and literary successors of Robert the Monk's crusaders; in Bernard's words they are 'the picked troops of God'.

---

31  Morris, pp. 94-95.

32  D. Carlson, 'Religious Writers', pp. 143-149.

33  Bernard of Clairvaux, Ep. 376; *Sancti Bernardi Opera*, vol. 8, ed. J. Leclercq and H.M. Rochais (Rome, 1977).

34  Robert the Monk, p. 765. See Riley-Smith, *First Crusade and the Idea of Crusading*, p. 148, where this passage is translated.

The fifth chapter of the treatise, *De Templo*, is in many ways the key element in its structure, since it serves as a transition from the first four chapters, which are concerned with the contrast between the Templars and the secular *malitia*, and the next eight chapters, in which Saint Bernard analyses the significance of the key sites in the Holy Land which it is the brothers' duty to protect. At the same time, Bernard sets down some of the central ecclesiastical conceptions about the nature of crusading in the first half of the twelfth century and, in doing so, prefigures his role in the preaching of the Second Crusade in 1147. Saint Bernard's new knighthood occupies the Temple of Solomon, a building which shines in its material splendour, whereas the Templars shine through their virtues. This is a typical bernardine perception. In his *Apologia* to William of Saint Thierry he castigates monasteries decorated with sculpture and painting, which may be necessary aids for a carnal laity, but should be eschewed by monks.[35] Not so for Suger of Saint Denis, his contemporary as abbot (1122-1151), whose lavish rebuilding of the abbey church was a conscious effort to contemplate God through material splendour, an opportunity to raise oneself from 'the slime of the earth' towards the immaterial. Indeed, Suger made overt comparison between his refurbishment of the church and the ornamentation of Hagia Sophia at Constantinople, details of which he gained from conversations with those who had travelled there from Jerusalem.[36] While Bernard and Suger were in complete agreement on the importance of ethical standards among contemporary knights,[37] their attitude towards the value of the material and terrestrial environment as a means of reaching towards the Divine is quite different. For Saint Bernard, the Templars,

---

35   Bernard of Clairvaux, 'Apologia ad Guillelmum Abbatem', cap. XII; SBOp 8:28-29.

36   *Abbot Suger on the Abbey Church of St-Denis and its Art Treasures*, ed., tr. and annotated by E. Panofsky, 2nd ed. G. Panofsky-Soergel (Princeton, N.J., 1979) pp. 64-65.

37   Suger, *Vie de Louis VI le Gros*, ed and tr. H. Waquet. Les classiques de l'Histoire de France au Moyen Age (Paris, 1929), for example, pp.134-135, 172-175. Grabois, 'Militia et Malitia: The Bernardine Vision of Chivalry' in *The Second Crusade and the Cistercians*, pp.52-54.

even though their functional role was the defence of the holy places, needed always to remember that ultimately the temporal glory of Jerusalem should not eclipse its heavenly counterpart, for 'the one is the figure of the other'. In the literal fulfilment of the liberation of Jerusalem, one should not be blind 'to the spiritual meaning of the texts'.

The Temple is, too, the site of the one act of violence in Christ's life, the driving out of the money-changers and sellers of doves who were defiling 'this house of prayer'. In the minds of Urban II and his twelfth-century successors, it was the Muslims who had polluted the holy places; Saint Bernard claimed that this pollution was far worse than that of the merchants. Equally, for Gregory VII the description of the expulsion of the money-changers had a special meaning, for Gregory, above all, was responsible for the creation of the idea of the *milites Christi* who could fight material battles on behalf of a holy cause.[38] Once Jerusalem had been captured, the news redounded throughout the world, reaching even the most remote islands. It was an occasion so momentous that it parallels the mission of the Apostles, sent out by Christ at the time of the Ascension. These events are brilliantly recorded on the great tympanum in the narthex at the abbey-church of Vézelay in northern Burgundy. Adolf Katzenellenbogen posits that the iconography here is the work of Peter the Venerable, abbot of Cluny, and another of Bernard's contemporaries, and that through it he is making conscious reference to the First Crusade as the beginning of a new christian mission following the past victories of Islam. It was on the hillside at Vézelay, in 1147, that Bernard tore up cloth to distribute as crosses for those pledged to take part in the expedition known as the Second Crusade.[39]

The Templars and the crusaders are then a specially chosen gen-

---

38   See I.S. Robinson, 'Gregory VII and the Soldiers of Christ', *History*, 58 (1973) 169-192.

39   A. Katzenellenbogen, 'The Central Tympanum at Vézelay: Its Encyclopedic Meaning and its Relation to the First Crusade', *Art Bulletin*, 26 (1944) 141-151.

eration. They are former sinners whom God has used to achieve his ends while at the same time providing them with the means of their own salvation. Saint Bernard is here taking up Urban II's vision of the crusade as it was glimpsed by those who recorded his speech at Clermont. By this means christian lands in the West, plagued by thieves, murderers, perjurers, and adulterers, can be cleansed of these people, while the former sinners themselves achieve salvation in their service in the holy warfare of the East, a situation quite unimaginable before God's gift of the holy war. Echoing Guibert of Nogent's assertion that a new way of salvation had been found for them, Bernard says that God has allowed Jerusalem to be besieged so often 'to furnish brave men an occasion for valor and immortality'. One of the many signs of the fertility of Jerusalem, which provides all manner of sustenance—both literal and spiritual—is that it offers 'a rich harvest of martyrs'. To suggest that he may be no more accurate here than in his stylised description of knights encumbered in battle by the long sleeves of their elaborate clothing does not detract from Bernard's rhetoric. Bernard knew well that most knights were not actually anarchic or gratuitously cruel, at least in their dealings with each other; it was rather that knightly and clerical perceptions of right behaviour started from quite different sets of assumptions. It has been suggested, moreover, that the diversion of leading secular nobles to the East had, in practice, quite the opposite effect, leaving a power vacuum to be exploited by criminal elements who had stayed at home. Many people must have been relieved to see the crusaders return.[40]

At the end of the chapter on the Temple, Bernard says that he is going to set out 'something of the delights in which you [that is, the Holy Land] abound'. This is not meant to be a pilgrim guide in the manner of those written by several pilgrim visitors in the course of the twelfth century,[41] for Bernard never himself visited

---

40  J. Riley-Smith, *The First Crusaders, 1095-1131* (Cambridge, 1997) pp. 145-146.

41  See the accounts collected in *Jerusalem Pilgrimage 1099-1185*, ed. J. Wilkinson, with J. Hill and W.F. Ryan, The Hakluyt Society, 167 (London, 1988).

Palestine and in fact, disapproved of monks who did. It is rather a vehicle for explaining the spiritual significance of these sites, the key being that of the Holy Sepulchre, upon which he expatiates at length. To the Templars, mostly adult knights with no monastic or spiritual training, it was important to convey the true meaning of their task in defending the holy places, particularly as they in turn might be called upon to explain this to others.[42] For the wider world the momentousness of the task which they had undertaken was surely justification for the creation of this new hybrid, the warrior-monk. In this section, Bernard was not building on Urban II's speech, for, in calling the crusade the pope had apparently made no attempt to exploit the potent attractions of the Holy Sepulchre. The abbot, however, recognised the great power that the holy places exercised over the imaginations of many western Christians and seized the opportunity to explain their full meaning to a receptive audience.[43] As Jean Leclercq remarked, 'there could be no clearer demonstration of the fact that [for Bernard] war is subordinate to these higher realities.'[44]

Bernard assigns a chapter each to Bethlehem, Nazareth, the Mount of Olives, and the Valley of Josaphat, the Jordan, Mount Calvary, the Holy Sepulchre, Bethphage, and Bethany, although nearly half of the survey is devoted to the Holy Sepulchre. The sequence is partly determined by the chronology of Christ's life rather than by any geographical coherence, and traces the significance of the places of his birth, childhood, baptism, death, and resurrection, ending with an analysis of the symbolism of Bethphage and of Bethany. By this means Bernard seems to be offering a theological interpretation of his earlier depiction of the role of knighthood. With Christ's first appearance at Bethlehem came 'the living bread' for 'the nourishment of holy

---

42  For Gillian Evans, *The Mind of St. Bernard* (Oxford, 1983) p. 29, his aim was to enable the Templars to look at these sites 'with spiritual eyes'. David Carlson, 'Practical Theology', p. 138, has a similar explanation, that these chapters offered the Templars 'a version of the *imitatio Christi* adapted for their particular needs'.

43  See also the comments of the Jean Richard, *The Crusades*, p. 481.

44  Leclercq, 'Saint Bernard's Attitude to War', p. 25.

souls'. He draws out the significance for the Templars who, no longer concerned with their own bodily comforts, as mature men have undertaken to devote themselves to Christ. 'He who has found life in the words of Christ no longer seeks the flesh.' Nazareth was where the infant God grew to maturity, 'as the fruit matures within the flower'. The inner truth then is covered by the outer garment, as the Templars' inner motivation lies beneath their exterior actions of fighting with the Muslims. Looking east from their quarters in the Temple, the brothers could see the valley of Josaphat and the Mount of Olives. To climb the one it was necessary to descend into the other so that 'one may not forget the fear of judgement'. In the valley the proud are crushed; only the humble can descend there in safety. Pride, the quintessential characteristic of the secular, worldly knight, cannot escape its end. The only route to the mountain is to be reborn in Christ in the baptismal waters of the Jordan. On Calvary Christ made atonement for the sins of humankind, as those who fight and die for the Lord undertake this action as a penance, to atone for their own sins.

The centrality of the Holy Sepulchre to the duties and obligations of the Templars is undoubted, and Bernard devotes to this by far the longest single section in the treatise. By his life and death Christ taught us all how to live and die: 'to live in holiness and to die in confidence'. These observations were central to contemporary debates about the reasons for the incarnation of Christ, debates which, stimulated by Saint Anselm's *Cur Deus Homo*, had been in progress since the 1090s.[45] The Templars can be seen as men who had taken up a role for which Christ's life and death were the model, fighting for pure motives and dying as martyrs. The death of Christ gave humankind the gift of the remission of sins, attainable by those who undertook the tasks of the Lord on crusade or in the military order. Secular knights who spurned the opportunity die twice: once a voluntary spiritual death; and also an imposed physical death, ignoring the example given to them by Christ. For men who risked their lives almost on a daily basis, Bernard's meditation on the nature and consequences of death was particularly apposite.

---

45    Evans, pp. 152-153.

Bernard concludes with Bethphage and Bethany.   Bethphage symbolises confession in the double sense: the total commitment of a follower of Christ and a penitent who fully perceives past sins. Bethany represents the supreme virtue of obedience which this confession entails. Both themes had been given emphasis in the earlier chapters describing the transformation effected in life and death when a knight joined the Templars.[46] Christ himself was the model, preferring obedience 'to his very life', while the resuscitation of Lazarus at Bethany demonstrated the power of this virtue over life itself. By their lives and actions the Templars demonstrate this commitment, but they must not trust simply in their own qualities. In the end, they can prevail only by God's strength and approval. The Templars therefore both defend these holy places by their physical presence and embody the virtues which each of these places symbolise.

Saint Bernard's support was invaluable to the Templars. His treatise clearly influenced Innocent II who in his major privilege to the order, *Omne Datum Optimum*, of 1139, evidently picks up the same themes. At the same time, the aristocratic world responded to the new Order with enthusiasm, providing land, income, and manpower on such a scale that, by the mid-century, the Temple had a major network of preceptories across Western Christendom, and through it was able to sustain its increasing responsibilities in the Latin states in the East. Even so, the doubts of those referred to by 'Hugh the Sinner' were never entirely dispelled, as Richard de Templo shows. For many the fundamental incompatibility of the cloister and the sword remained integral to their perceptions of the world. Among others, such diverse personalities as John of Salisbury, Isaac of Stella, abbot of L'Etoile in Poitou, and Walter Map, archdeacon of Oxford, have left critical commentaries on the functions of these warrior-monks,[47] criticisms which, ultimately, would resurface at the vital time of the Templars' trial in the early fourteenth century.

46  Carlson, 'Practical Theology', p. 139.

47  See Barber, pp. 59-63.

# TRANSLATOR'S NOTE

BERNARD OF CLAIRVAUX never visited the Holy Land, and did not apparently approve of monks who did. 'It is evident,' he wrote, 'that what is needed there are soldiers to fight rather than monks to pray'.[1]  Yet the sons of Saint Bernard did establish monasteries in the land where Christ had lived and taught, most recently in the valley of Ayallon—where Joshua made the sun stand still, and where that same sun still smiles on the richest vineyards in the East.

On the hill overlooking the monastery stand the ruins of a thirteenth-century crusader's castle, built by the same Templars for whom this treatise was written; and some half mile up the valley is Emmaus—or at least one of the sites identified as Emmaus— where Christ broke bread with his disciples on the evening of the first Easter. It was here that this translation was made.

The work of translating one of Bernard's better polished literary productions has been a real pleasure, and in doing it, I have followed the guidelines and general principles set down for the other treatises in this series.

May the earthly Jerusalem which Bernard never saw, but on whose soil his sons and successors are privileged to tread, continue to be the figure of that heavenly Jerusalem, our mother, to which Bernard so ardently aspired![2]

Latroun, Israel                    M. Conrad Greenia OCSO

---

1  Bernard, Ep 355; SBOp 7:299; PL 182:337; BSJ, Ep 275, p. 348; and Ep 253; SBOp 7:149-155; PL 182:453; BSJ, Ep 328, p. 404. See also Vita Bern 3:22; PL 185:316.

2  See below, 5.11.

1   2 Tim 2:3. The usual translation of *miles* is 'soldier', but 'knight' seems more suitable. On Hugh of Payens or Payns, see Jean Richard, 'Le milieu familial' in *Bernard de Clairvaux*, Commission d'Histoire de l'Ordre de Cîteaux (Paris: Alsatia, 1953) 13-14.

2   2 Tim 4:7.

3   In 'Un document sur les débuts des Templiers' in *Revue d'histoire ecclésiastique* 52 (1957) pp. 81-91, Jean Leclercq edits a letter which he urges as being written by Hugh of Payens and giving the background for this exhortation and defense on the part of Saint Bernard. However, C. Sclafert in his 'Lettre inédite de Hughes de Saint-Victor aux chevaliers du Temple' in *Revue d'ascetique et de mystique* 34 (1958) pp. 275-299, gives cogent arguments for attributing the letter to Hugh of Saint Victor. Leclercq republished his article, unchanged, in *Recueil d'études sur saint Bernard et ses écrits*, 2 (Rome: Edizioni di Storia e Letteratura, 1966) 87-99, adding at the end a 'Postscriptum' in which he notes Father Sclafert's article and concludes (p. 99): '. . . l'attribution à Hugues de Saint-Victor est les plus vraisemblable.'.

4   Leclercq, *Recueil* 2:98, sees in the imagery Bernard uses here an indication that he is writing a defence.

# PROLOGUE

IF I AM NOT MISTAKEN, my dear Hugh, you have asked me not once or twice, but three times to write a few words of exhortation for you and your comrades.[3] You say that, while I am not permitted to wield the lance, I might at least brandish my pen against a tyrannical foe, and that this moral, rather than material, support of mine will be of no small help to you.[4] I have put you off now for quite some time, not because I scorn your request, but for fear I may be blamed for accepting lightly and hastily, or that I may botch a task which might better be done by a more qualified hand and which might, because of me, still remain just as requisite and that much more difficult.

Having waited quite some time to no purpose, I have now done what I could, lest inability be mistaken for unwillingness. It is for the reader to judge the result. Although some may find my work unsatisfactory or short of the mark, I shall be nonetheless content, for I have not failed to give you my best.

# CHAPTER ONE

## A WORD OF EXHORTATION
## FOR THE KNIGHTS OF THE TEMPLE

A NEW KIND OF KNIGHTHOOD seems recently to have appeared on the earth, and in that part of the world which the Orient from on high once visited in the flesh.[1] As he then drove out the powers of darkness by the strength of his mighty hand,[2] so he now drives out their supporters, the children of disbelief,[3] scattering them by the hand of his mighty.[4] Even now he brings about the redemption of his people,[5] and again raises up for us a horn of salvation in the house of his servant David.[6]

This, I repeat, is a new kind of knighthood and one unknown in ages past. It indefatigably wages a twofold combat, against flesh and blood and against a spiritual hosts of evil in the heavens.[7] When someone bravely resists a physical foe, relying solely on physical strength, I find this hardly astounding, since this is not uncommon. And when war is waged by spiritual strength against vices or demons, this, too, is nothing remarkable, though I consider it praiseworthy, for the world is full of monks.[8] But for a

---

1     Lk 1:78.

2     Eph 6:12; Is 10:13.

3     Eph 2:2.

4     Nahum 2:5.

5     Lk 1:68.

6     Lk 1:69.

7     Eph 6:12.

8     On the explosion of monastic life in the eleventh and twelfth ceturies, see, for example, Peter King, *Western Monasticism* (Kalamazoo, 1999) Chapters 7-8.

man powerfully to gird himself[9] with both swords[10] and nobly
mark his belt[11] —who would not consider this very worthy of great
admiration, even more so since it has hitherto been unknown?
Truly a fearless knight and secure on every side is he whose soul
is protected by the armor of faith[12] just as his body is protected
by armor of steel. Doubly armed, surely, he need fear neither
demons nor men. Not that he fears death—no, he desires it. Why
should he fear to live or to die when for him *to live is Christ, and
to die is gain?*[13] Gladly and faithfully he stands up for Christ, but
he would prefer to be dissolved and to be with Christ,[14] by far the
better thing.

March forth confidently then, you knights, and with a stalwart
heart repel the foes of the cross of Christ.[15] Be sure that neither
death nor life can separate you from the love of God which is in
Jesus Christ.[16] In every peril repeat, '*Whether we live or whether
we die, we are the Lord's*'. [17] How gloriously victors return from
battle! How blessedly martyrs die in battle! Rejoice, brave athlete,
if you live and conquer in the Lord; but glory and exult still more
if you die and join your Lord. Life is indeed fruitful and victory
glorious, but more important than either is a holy death. If they
are blessed who die in the Lord,[18] how much more so are those
who die for the Lord!

2. Precious indeed in the sight of the Lord is the death of his holy

---

9    Ps 44:4. (The Vulgate-Douay enumeration is followed for the Psalms as
     being the one with which Bernard was familiar.)

10   Lk 22:38. See Ep 256; SBOp 8:161-162; PL 182:463-4654; BSJ; Ep 399,
     pp. 470-472; and Csi 4:7; SBOp 3:454, for Bernard's doctrine on the
     two swords.

11   I.e., with the cross.

12   I Thess 5:8.

13   Phil 1:21.

14   Phil 1:23.

15   Phil 3:18.

16   Rom 3:38.

17   Rom 14:8.

18   Rev 14:13.

ones,[19] whether they die in battle or in bed, but death in battle is more precious as it is more glorious. How secure life is when the conscience is pure! How secure I say, life is, when death is regarded without fear; indeed, when it is anticipated with composure and accepted with reverence! How truly holy and secure this knighthood and how entirely free of the double risk run by the kind of men who are often at risk, but who do not fight for Christ's cause! Whenever you march out, o worldly warrior, you have to worry that killing your foe's body may mean killing your soul, or that by him you may be killed, body and soul both.

Indeed, danger or victory for the Christian are weighed by the focus of the heart, not the fortunes of war. If he fights for a good cause, the outcome of the battle can never be evil; and likewise the result can never be considered good if the cause is evil and the intention unrighteous. If you happen to be killed while you intend to kill another, you die a murderer. If you prevail and by your intention of overcoming and conquering you perhaps kill a man, you live a murderer. Yet to be a murderer, whether living or dead, victorious or vanquished, is not a good thing. What an unhappy victory—to have conquered a man while yielding to vice. And if anger or arrogance have got the best of you, in vain do you boast over the fallen enemy.

But what of those who kill neither in the fury of vengeance nor the frenzy of conquest, but simply in self-defence? Even this sort of victory I would not call a good victory, since of the two, physical death is a lesser evil than spiritual. The soul need not die when the body is slain. No, it is the soul which sins that shall die.[20]

---

19   Ps 115:15.

20   Ezek 18:4.

# CHAPTER TWO

## ON WORLDLY KNIGHTHOOD

WHAT THEN IS THE GOAL OR THE FRUIT of this worldly–I will call it, not knighthood, but–knavery? What if not the mortal sin of the victor and the eternal death of the vanquished? Well then, to borrow a word from the Apostle, *let someone who plows, plow in hope, and someone who threshes, do so in view of garnering the grain.*[1]

What then, O knights, is this stupendous misapprehension and what this unbearable impulse which bids you fight with such pomp and pains, and all to no purpose save death and sin? You drape your horses in silk, and plume your armor with I know not what sort of rags; you paint your shields and your saddles; you adorn your bits and spurs with gold and silver and precious stones, and then in all this pomp, with shameful wrath and fearless folly, you charge to your death. Are these the trappings of a warrior or are they not rather the trinkets of a woman? Do you think the swords of your foes will be deflected by your gold, spare your jewels or fail to pierce your silks?

As you yourselves have often certainly experienced, there are three things especially needful to a warrior: a knight must guard his person with vigor, shrewdness, and caution; he must be unimpeded in his movements, and he must be quick to draw his sword. You, by contrast, blind yourselves with effeminate tresses and trip yourselves up with long, voluminous tunics, burying your tender, delicate hands in cumbersome, flowing sleeves. Over and above all this, there is that terrible insecurity of conscience, in spite of all your armor, since you have dared to under-

---

1   1 Cor 9:10.

take so dangerous a business on such slight and frivolous grounds. Nothing stirs you to battle or rouses you to disputes, really, except flashes of irrational anger, hunger for empty glory,[2] or hankering after some earthly possessions? For causes like these It certainly is not safe to kill or to be killed.

---

2    Gal 5:26.

# CHAPTER THREE

## ON THE NEW KNIGHTHOOD

BUT THE KNIGHTS OF CHRIST may safely do battle in the battles of their Lord, fearing neither the sin of smiting the enemy nor the danger of their own downfall, inasmuch as death for Christ, inflicted or endured, bears no taint of sin, but deserves abundant glory. In the first case one gains for Christ, and in the second one gains Christ himself, who freely accepts the death of the foe in vengeance, and yet more freely gives himself in consolation to his fallen knight.

The knight of Christ,[1] I say, may strike with confidence and succumb more confidently. When he strikes, he does service to Christ, and to himself when he succumbs. Nor does he bear the sword in vain. He is God's minister[2] in the punishment of evil doers and the praise of well doers.[3] Surely, if he kills an evil doer, he is not a man-killer, but, if I may so put it, an evil-killer. Clearly he is reckoned the avenger of Christ against evildoers,[4] and the defender of Christians. Should he be killed himself, we know he has not perished, but has come safely home. The death which he inflicts is Christ's gain, and that which he suffers, his own.[5] At the death of the pagan, the Christian exults because Christ is exalted; in the death of the Christian the King's liberality is conspicuous when the knight is ushered home to be rewarded. In the one case

---

2 Tim 2:3.

Rom 13:4.

1 Pet 2:14.

Rom 13:4.

Phil 1:21.

a just person shall rejoice at regarding vindication;[6] in the other man shall say, *Truly there is a reward for the just; truly it is God who judges the earth.*[7]

Yet this is not to say that the pagans are to be slaughtered when there is any other way of preventing them from harassing and persecuting the faithful; but only that now it seems better to destroy them than to allow the rod of sinners to continue to be raised over the lot of the righteous, lest perchance the righteous set their hand to iniquity.[8]

5. What then? If it is never legitimate for a Christian to strike with the sword, why then did the Saviour's precursor bid soldiers be content with their pay,[9] and not rather ban military service to them? But if, as is the case, it is legitimate for all those ordained to it by the Almighty—provided they have not embraced a higher calling—then to whom, I ask, may it more rightly be allowed than to those into whose hands and hearts is committed on behalf of all of us Sion, the city of our strength?[10] So that once the transgressors of divine law have been expelled, the righteous nation that preserves the truth may enter in surety.[11]

Surely then the nations who choose warfare should be scattered,[12] those who molest us should be cut away,[13] and all the workers of iniquity should be dispersed from the city of the Lord[14]—those who busy themselves carrying off the incalculable riches placed in Jerusalem by christian people, profaning holy things[15] and pos-

---

6   Ps 57:11

7   Ps 57:12.

8   Ps 124:3.

9   Lk 3:14. The Precursor is John the Baptist.

10   Is 26:1.

11   Is 26:2.

12   Ps 67:31.

13   Gal 5:12.

14   Ps 100:8.

15   Lev 19:8.

sessing the sanctuary of God as their heritage.[16] Let both swords[17] of the faithful fall upon the necks of the foe to the destruction of every lofty thing lifting itself up against the knowledge of God[18] which is the christian faith, *lest the Gentiles should then say, 'Where is their God?'*[19]

6. Once they have been cast out, He shall return to his heritage and to his house, of which he said in anger in the Gospel, *Behold, your house will be left to you desolate.*[20] And through the Prophet he had complained: I have left my house, *I have forsaken my heritage.*[21] And he will fulfill that other prophecy: *The Lord has ransomed his people and delivered them.*[22] *They shall come to Mount Sion and exult, and rejoice in the good things of the Lord.'*[23]

Rejoice Jerusalem,[24] and recognize right now the time of your visitation![25] Be glad and give praise all at once, wastelands of Jerusalem, for the Lord has comforted his people. He has ransomed Jerusalem. The Lord has bared his holy arm in the sight of all the nations.[26] O virgin Israel, you had fallen and there was no one to raise you up.[27] Rise up now and shake off the dust, O virgin, captive daughter of Sion.[28] Rise up, I say, and stand on high. Look at the happiness which is coming to you from your

---

16  Ps 82:13.

17  Lk 22:38. See above, chapter 1, note 10.

18  2 Cor 10:4-5.

19  Ps 113:2.

20  Mt 23:38.

21  Jer 12:7.

22  Ps 76:16.

23  Jer 31:11-12. Bernard has fused this passage with the above text from Ps 76.

24  Is 66:10. Introit for the Fourth Sunday of Lent.

25  Lk 19:44.

26  Is 52:9-10.

27  Amos 5:2.

28  Is 52:2.

God.[29] You will no longer be referred to as forsaken, nor your land any more be termed a wilderness, for the Lord has taken delight in you, and your land shall be peopled.[30] Raise your eyes, look around you and see; all these have gathered together and come to you.[31] This is help sent to you by the Holy One![32] Through them already is fulfilled the ancient promise, *I will make you the pride of the ages, a joy from generation to generation. You will suck the milk of the nations and be nourished at the breasts of kings.*[33] And again, *As a mother consoles her children, so will I console you, and in Jerusalem you will be consoled.*[34]

Do you not see how often these ancient witnesses authorize the new knighthood? Surely, what we have heard, we have now seen in the city of the Lord of hosts.[35] At the same time, of course, we must not let this literal interpretation blind us to the spiritual meaning of the texts,[36] for we must live in eternal hope in spite of such temporal realizations of prophetic utterances. Otherwise what is beheld would supplant what is believed, material penury threaten spiritual wealth[37] and present possessions void future fulfillment. What is more, the temporal glory of the earthly city does not demolish its heavenly rewards, but demonstrates them, at

---

29  Bar 4:36; 5:5. Communion verse for the Second Sunday of Advent in the Roman Missal.

30  Is 62:4.

31  Is 49:18.

32  Ps 19:3.

33  Is 60:15-16.

34  Is 66:13.

35  Ps 47:9.

36  On the various sense of Scripture and their use by the Fathers, see Henri de Lubac, *Exégèse Médiéval*, 4 vols. (Paris: Aubier, 1959-1964). Translated as *Medieval Exegesis* by Mark Sebanc (Grand Rapids: Eerdmans-Edinburgh: T. & T. Clark) Volume 1 (1998).

37  On the cistercian ideal of poverty, see, for example, Guerric of Igny, Sermon 53.5 for All Saints Day (CF 32:209): 'What I have said is not new to you, my brethren, but I still want to impress upon you that truly blessed poverty of spirit is to be found more in humility of heart than in a mere privation of everyday possessions,and it consists more in the renunciation of pride than in a mere contempt for property. Sometimes it may be useful to own things . . . .'

least so long as we remember that the one is the figure of the other, and that it is the heavenly which is our mother.[38]

---

38   Gal 4:26.

# CHAPTER FOUR

## ON THE LIFESTYLE
## OF THE KNIGHTS OF THE TEMPLE

**A**ND NOW AS AN EXEMPLAR, or at least an embarrassment, for those of our knights who are apparently fighting not for God, but for the devil, we will briefly set forth the life and virtues of these knights of Christ: how they conduct themselves at home as well as in battle, how they appear in public, and how the knighthood of God and of the world differ from the one another.[1]

First, discipline is in no way lacking, and obedience is never despised. As Scripture testifies, *the undisciplined son shall perish,*[2] and *rebellion is as much a sin as witchcraft, to refuse obedience is like the crime of idolatry.*[3] They come and they go at the bidding of their superior.[4] They wear what he gives them[5] and do not presume to wear or to eat anything from another source.[6] Both in raiment and in rations[7] they shun every excess and have regard only for what is necessary. They live in cheerful community and sober company, without wives and without children. So that their evangelical perfection will lack nothing, they dwell united in one

---

[1]  The *Rule of the Knights Templar* has been edited by H. de Curzon, *La Règle du Temple, Société de l'Histoire de France* (Paris 1856). See also PL 166:853-873 and G. Schnürer, *Die Ursprüngliche Templerregel* (Freiburg-im-Breisgau, 1903) 129-153. A new critical edition is in preparation.

[2]  Sir 22:3.

[3]  1 Sam 15:23.

[4]  Lk 7:8.

[5]  RB 55.

[6]  Cf. RB 51.

[7]  Cf. RB 29.7-9.

family[8] with no personal property whatever,[9] careful to keep the unity of the Spirit in the bond of peace.[10] You may say that the whole multitude has but one heart and one soul[11] to the point that no one follows his own will, but seeks instead to follow the commander.[12]

They never sit in idleness or wander about aimlessly,[13] but on the rare occasions when they are not on duty, they are always careful to earn their bread[14] by repairing their worn armor and torn clothing, or simply by setting things to order. For the rest, they are guided by the common needs and by the will of their master.[15]

There is little distinction of persons among them,[16] and deference is shown to ability, not to nobility.[17] They rival one another in mutual consideration,[18] and they carry one another's burdens, thus fulfilling the law of Christ.[19] No arrogant word, no idle deed, no unrestrained laugh, not even the slightest whisper or murmur, is left uncorrected once it has been detected.[20] They foreswear dice and chess, they abhor the hunt; they take no delight, as is customary, in the ridiculous cruelty of falconry. Jesters, wizards, bards, bawdy minstrels and jousters, they despise and reject as so many vanities and deceitful follies.[21] They cut their hair short, cognizant that, according to the Apostle, it is

---

8    Ps 67:7.
9    RB 55.16-18.
10   Eph 4:3.
11   Acts 4:32.
12   RB 4.60-61.
13   Cf. RB 48.1.
14   2 Thes 3:8.
15   RB 48.3, 11.
16   Rom 2:11.
17   RB 2.20-22; 63.1,7-8.
18   Rom 12:10; RB 72.4.
19   Gal 6:2.
20   RB 4.7.
21   Ps 39:5.

shameful for a man to cultivate flowing locks.[22] They never dress, and seldom wash,[23] their hair—content to let it appear tousled and dusty, darkened by chain mail and heat.

8. When a battle is at hand, they arm themselves interiorly with faith and exteriorly with steel rather than with gold. Thus armed and not embellished, they strike fear rather than incite greed in the enemy. They seek out strong, swift horses, rather than those which are dappled and well-plumed. They set their minds on fighting to win rather than on parading for show. They take no thought for glory but seek to be formidable rather than flamboyant. Then, too, they are not quarrelsome, reckless, or impulsively foolhardy, but they draw up their ranks deliberately, prudently, and providently, arraying themselves in the line of battle as we read about in the Fathers.[24] Indeed, the true Israelites[25] march into battle as men of peace.[26]

Yet once in the thick of battle, they set aside this earlier gentleness, as if to say, *Do I not hate those who hate you, O Lord; am I not disgusted with your enemies?*'[27] These men charge the enemy, regarding the foe as sheep, never—no matter how outnumbered they are—as ruthless barbarians or as awesome hordes. Nor do they presume on their own strength,[28] but trust for victory in the Lord of Saboath.[29] They are mindful of the words of Maccabees, *It is simple enough for a multitude to be vanquished by a handful. It makes no difference in the sight of the God of heaven whether he grants deliverance by the hands of few or of many; for victory in war does not depend on a big army, but bravery is the gift from heaven.*'[30]

---

22   1 Cor 11:14.

23   RB 36.8.

24   2 Mac 12:20; see also 8:23 and 1 Mac 4:41.

25   Jn 1:47.

26   Gen 42:31; Mt 5:9.

27   Ps 138:21.

28   Judg 7:2.

29   2 Mac 15:8; Jer 11:20.

30   1 Mac 3:18-19.

As they have on numerous occasions experienced, one man may pursue a thousand, and two put ten thousand to flight.[31]

Thus in an astounding and unique manner they appear gentler than lambs, yet fiercer than lions. Consequently, I do not know if it would be more appropriate to refer to them as monks or as soldiers, or whether it would perhaps be better to recognize them as being both, for they lack neither monastic meekness nor military might. What can we say about this, except that this is the Lord's doing, and it is marvelous in our eyes.[32] God has hand picked such troops, and from among the most valiant men of Israel he recruited from the ends of the earth servants to guard vigilantly and faithfully that sepulchre which is the bed of the true Solomon; all bearing sword in hand, and superbly trained to war.[33]

---

31   Deut 32:30; 2 Mac 8:19-20.
32   Ps 117:23.
33   Song 3:7-8.

# CHAPTER FIVE

## THE TEMPLE OF JERUSALEM

I N THE VERY TEMPLE OF JERUSALEM, they have their quarters. It is not as splendid as the ancient and highly celebrated temple of Solomon, yet no less glorious. What is more, all the magnificence of the first temple lay in perishable gold and silver,[1] in polished stones and precious woods;[2] whereas all the beauty and gracious, charming adornment of its present counterpart is the religious fervor of its occupants and their well-disciplined behavior. In the former, one could contemplate all sorts of beautiful colors, while in the latter, one is able to venerate all sorts of virtues and good works. Holiness indeed suits the house of God;[3] it delights, not in burnished marble, but in polished manners, and loves pure minds far more than gilt paneling.

The facade of this temple is adorned, of course, but with weapons rather than jewels, and in place of the ancient golden crowns, it walls are hung round with shields.[4] In place of candlesticks, censers, and ewers, this house is well furnished with saddles, bridles, and lances. By all these signs the knights clearly show that they are animated by the same zeal for the house of God which of old vehemently inflamed the Leader of knighthood himself, who, having his most sacred hands armed, not with a weapon, but with a whip which he had fashioned from lengths of cord, entered the temple, ousted the merchants, scattered the coins of the money changers, and overturned the chairs of the pigeon vendors, considering it totally unfitting to defile this house of prayer by such traffic.[5]

---

1   1 Pet 1:18.

2   1 Kings 6ff.

3   Ps 92:5.

4   1 Mac 4:57.

5   Mt 21:12-13, Jn 2:14-16.

Moved therefore by their King's example, his devoted soldiery, considering it far more unfitting and infinitely more intolerable for a holy place to be polluted by unbelievers[6] than to be crowded with merchants, have installed themselves in this holy house with their horses and their armour.  Having expunged it and the other holy places of every infidel stain and the tyrannical horde, they occupy themselves day and night with work as distinguished as it is practical. They honor the temple of God earnestly with fervent and sincere worship, in their devotion offering up, not the flesh of animals according to the ancient rites,[7] but true peace offerings, brotherly love, devoted obedience, and voluntary poverty.

10. These events at Jerusalem have shaken the world. The islands hearken, and the people from afar give ear.[8] They swarm forth from East and West, as a flood stream bringing glory to the nations[9] and a rushing river gladdening the city of God.[10] What could be perceived as more pleasant and deemed more suitable than seeing so great a multitude of men thronging to reinforce the few—unless it is seeing along them godless rogues, sacrilegious thieves, murderers, perjurers, and adulterers?[11] At their departure, there is a twofold joy and a twofold benefit: their countrymen are as glad to be rid of them as their new comrades are to receive them. Both sides have profited from this exchange; one group gains protection and the other gets rid of a nuisance. Thus Egypt rejoices in their departure[12] while in their protection Mount Sion rejoices no less and the daughters of Judah are glad.[13] The former glory in being delivered from their hands,[14] while the

---

6   Lev 19:8.

7   1 Kings 8:63.

8   Is 49:1.

9   Is 66:12.

10   Ps 45:5.

11   1 Tim 1:9-10

12   Ps 104:38; Ex 12:33, 36. *Profectus* here has a double meaning: conversion and departure.

13   Ps 47:12.

14   Lk 1:74.

latter have every reason to expect deliverance by means of these same hands. The former gladly see their ruthless despoilers depart, while the latter gladly welcome staunch defenders. In the process, the one gets very welcome reinforcements, while the other gets some equally beneficial relief.

This is the revenge Christ contrives against his enemies,[15] to triumph powerfully and gloriously over them by their own means. Surely it is both happy and fitting that those who have so long fought against him should at last begin to fight for him. He recruits his soldiers among his foes, just as once he turned Saul the persecutor into Paul the preacher.[16] For this reason, I would not be surprised if, as our Saviour himself has affirmed, the court of heaven is taking more joy in one sinner who repents than in the many just persons who have no need of repentance.[17] Certainly the conversion of so many sinners and evil doers will now do as much good as their former conduct did harm.

11. Hail then, holy city,[18] which the Most High has sanctified to himself as his own tabernacle,[19] by which in you and through you this generation might be saved! Hail, city of the great King,[20] source of new and joyous and unheard of marvels! Hail mistress of nations and prince of provinces,[21] province of patriarchs,[22] mother of apostles and prophets, cradle of the faith and glory of the christian people! From earliest times God has permitted you to be continually besieged, so that to persons brave and virtuous you might provide the opportunity for salvation.

Hail promised land, flowing once upon a time with milk and

---

15  Nahum 1:2.

16  Acts 9:1-22.

17  Lk 15:7.

18  Is 52:1.

19  Ps 45:5.

20  Ps 47:3.

21  Lam 1:1.

22  Gen 17:8.

honey for your ancient inhabitants,[23] and now with healing grace
and vital sustenance for the whole earth! A good land, I say, the
best, which, receiving into your ever fruitful womb the heavenly
grain from the heart of the eternal Father[24] has from that super-
nal seed brought forth a rich harvest of martyrs. And from among
the rest of the faithful throughout the world, your fertile soil has
produced no less fruit—some thirtyfold, some sixty, and some a
hundredfold.[25] Happily filled and lavishly fattened on the great
abundance of your sweetness, those who have seen you are replete
with your munificent bounty.[26] Everywhere they go, even to the
ends of the earth,[27] they burble over with the memory of your
abundant goodness[28] and they speak of the splendors of your
glory[29] to those who have never seen you, telling of the marvels
which are being accomplished in you[30]. Glorious things are spoken of you, city of God![31] Now then we will note down some few
of the delights in which you abound, for the praise and glory of
your name.

---

23  Ex 3:8.

24  Lk 8:15.

25  Mt 13:23.

26  Ps 30:20. Literally, belch the memory of your munificent bounty.

27  Is 49:6. See also, Acts 1:8, 13:47.

28  Ps 144:7.

29  Ps 144:5.

30  Sir 36:10.

31  Ps 86:3.

# CHAPTER SIX

## BETHLEHEM

**B**EFORE ALL ELSE for the nourishment of holy souls[1] you have Bethlehem, the house of bread. It was there he first appeared——he, the living bread come down from heaven,[2] born of the Virgin. There to docile draft animals is shown the crib,[3] and in the crib the straw from the virgin field; and there the ox may recognize his owner, and the ass the manger of his Lord.[4] All flesh is grass, of course, and all its glory is as the wildflower.[5] But man, having failed to understand the honor in which he was made, has been likened to the dumb beasts, and made like them.[6] The Word, the Bread of Angels, has become the fodder of animals so that the flesh, which had become quite unused to eating the bread of the Word, might have grass to ruminate until through the God-man having been returned to its prior dignity and converted from being a beast again into being a man, it may say with Saint Paul, *Although we have known Christ according to the flesh, we know him so no longer.*[7]

This I think nobody can truly say unless he has with Peter first heard from the mouth of Truth this other saying, *The words which I have spoken to you are spirit and life, but the flesh is of no profit.*[8] Someone who has found life in the words of Christ no

---

1   Wis 3:13.

2   Jn 6:51.

3   Lk 2:7.

4   Is 1:3.

5   Is 40:6.

6   Ps 48:13.

7   2 Cor 5:16.

8   Jn 6:64.

longer seeks the flesh[9] but is now one of the number of the blessed who believe without seeing.[10] Only a child needs a cup of milk,[11] and only an animal hay fodder.[12] But someone who does not offend in word is a full grown man,[13] capable of taking solid food.[14] Albeit by the sweat of his brow,[15] he eats the bread of the Word without revulsion. Secure and without scandal he will speak the wisdom of God when he is in the company of full grown men,[16] comparing spiritual truths with spiritual persons.[17] Yet when he is with children or the beasts of the herd, he will be careful to adjust himself to their capacity, and to speak only of Christ and him crucified.[18]

Yet it is one and the same sweet nourishment from the heavenly pastures which furnishes fodder for animals to ruminate and bread for men to eat, a source of strength for adults and of growth for the immature.

---

9    Prov 8:35.
10   Jn 20:29.
11   1 Cor 3:2.
12   Ps 103:14.
13   Jas 3:2.
14   Heb 5:14.
15   Gen 3:19.
16   1 Cor 2:6.
17   1 Cor 2:13.
18   1 Cor 2:2.

# CHAPTER SEVEN

## NAZARETH

THERE, TOO, ONE MAY SEE NAZARETH, which means, the flower. It was here the infant God born in Bethlehem grew to maturity, as the fruit matures within the flower, so that the scent of the flower may precede the savor of the fruit, and the holy liquor seep from the nostrils of the prophets to the throat of the apostles. The Jews had to content themselves with an ephemeral perfume, while Christians might nourish themselves on solid food. Nathanael indeed perceived this flower whose scent was sweeter than any ointment.[1] This is why he asked, *Can anything good come from Nazareth?*[2] Not content with the scent alone, he accepted Philip's invitation to come and see.[3] In fact, he was already captivated by the whiff of this wondrous sweetness and made more eager to taste the fruit by inhaling its fragrance. Drawn on by the odor, he took pains to arrive at the fruit without delay. He wanted to experience more fully what he had as yet only faintly sensed, and taste what he had sniffed from afar.

Let us see if we can not perhaps shed some small light on this passage by comparing it to the sense of smell of Isaac [the patriarch]. Scripture says of him that, *As soon as he caught the scent of his garments* (meaning of course, his son Jacob), he said, '*Behold, the odor of my son is like the odor of a fruitful field which the Lord has blessed.*'[4] He caught the scent of the garments, but he did not recognize the person wearing them. Delighted exteriorly by the

---

1    Song 4:10.
2    Jn 1:46.
3    *Ibid.*
4    Gen 27:27.

mere odor of these garments, as if of a flower, he did not, as it were, taste the sweetness of the interior fruit, and he remained deceived in recognizing the sacred destiny for which this son had been chosen.[5]

What is the meaning of all this? The garment is clearly the spirit of the Word, and the letter his flesh. But now the Jews are not able to recognize either the Word in flesh, the divinity in man, or the spiritual sense hidden beneath the written word. They feel only the goat skin covering which resembles the elder brother,[6] that is, the first and ancient sinner [Adam], and are not able to arrive at the naked truth. Not in the flesh of sin, but in the likeness of the flesh of sin'[7]—for he could not commit sin,[8] but came to take sin away[9]—he appeared for the reason he never concealed, *so that the blind might see, and the clear–sighted might become blind.*[10]

By this likeness [11] the deluded prophet and the blind of our day bless him whom they do not know.[12] Although they read of him in their books,[13] they fail to recognize him in his mighty deeds. They have touched him with their own hands,[14] bound him,[15] scourged him[16] and buffeted him,[17] but without realizing that he was to rise from the dead.[18] If they had known, they would never have crucified the Lord of glory.[19]

---

5    Gen 25:23.
6    Gen 27:22-23.
7    Rom 8:3.
8    1 Pet 2:22.
9    Jn 1:29.
10    Jn 9:39.
11    Gen 27:27.
12    Jn 4:22.
13    2 Cor 3:15.
14    Gen 27:12.
15    Jn 18:12.
16    Jn 19:1.
17    Mt 26:67.
18    Jn 2:20-21.
19    1 Cor 2:8.

We will say a few words about the other holy places—if not all of them, then at least some. Our incapacity obliges us to leave much unsaid but at least we may speak briefly about some of their more striking aspects.

# CHAPTER EIGHT

## THE MOUNT OF OLIVES
## AND THE VALLEY OF JOSAPHAT

TO CLIMB THE MOUNT OF OLIVES one must go down into the valley of Josaphat, so that in contemplating the richness of divine mercy you may not forget the fear of judgment. If in the abundance of his mercy he is always inclined to forgive,[1] his judgments are nonetheless exceedingly deep[2] and acknowledged to be utterly terrifying to the sons of men.[3] David it is who shows us the Mount of Olives, saying, *You rescue both man and beast, O Lord, in the generous outpouring of your mercy.*'[4] He refers in the same psalm to the valley of judgment, saying, *Let not the foot of pride approach me, nor let the hands of sinners shake me.*[5] He even admits his dread of sharing their lot, when, in another psalm, he says in prayer, *Pierce my flesh with your fear; indeed I am afraid of your judgments.*[6]

Into this valley the proud stumble and are crushed; the humble descend and suffer little harm. The proud man excuses his sin, but the humble man accuses himself, knowing that God will not judge him a second time,[7] and that if we judge ourselves we shall assuredly escape judgment.[8]

---

1   Is 55:7.

2   Ps 35:7.

3   Ps 65:5.

4   Ps 35:7-8.

5   Ps 35:12.

6   Ps 118:120.

7   Nahum 1:9 (LXX).

8   1 Cor 11:31.

15. Furthermore, the proud man, paying no attention to how terrible it is to fall into the hands of the living God,[9] facilely breaks into excuses for his sins with words of malice.[10] It is indeed great malice not to have mercy on yourself and to reject the sole remedy of confessing after sinning. Instead of shaking off burning coals, you clasp them to your bosom,[11] and refuse to heed the advice of the Wise Man who said, Please God by having mercy on your own soul.[12] Besides, if someone does harm to himself, to whom will he do good?[13] Now the world is being judged, now the prince of this world is cast forth,[14] cast him forth from your heart, that is, if you judge yourself by humbling yourself. The judgment of heaven will take place when He calls the heavens from above, and the earth, too, that He may separate out his people.[15] Being cast out with the devil and his angels,[16] if you are found as yet unjudged—this is something to be afraid of.

On the other hand, the spiritual man who judges all things is himself judged by no one.[17] This is why judgment begins at the house of God,[18] so that at his coming the Judge shall discover that his followers, whom he recognizes,[19] have already been judged. And then he will have nothing further to judge against them when he comes to judge those who labor not as common men and suffer not from the common scourges.[20]

---

9    Heb 10:31.
10   Ps 140:4.
11   Prov 6:27.
12   Sir 30:24.
13   Sir 14:5.
14   Jn 12:31.
15   Ps 49:4.
16   Mt 25:41.
17   1 Cor 2:15.
18   1 Pet 4:17.
19   Jn 10:14; 13:18.
20   Ps 72:5.

# CHAPTER NINE

## THE JORDAN

HOW JOYFULLY the Jordan clasps Christians in its embrace—that river which glories in having been sanctified by the baptism of Christ! Certainly that syrian leper was deceived in preferring some unknown waters of Damascus to the waters of Israel,[1] when those of our river Jordan have been utterly proven, consecrated, and submissive to God—whether when they miraculously parted to leave a dry path for Elijah and for Elisha,[2] or in an earlier age for Joshua and for all the people.[3] Furthermore, what river can claim pre-eminence over the one which the Trinity has dedicated to itself by its manifest presence? The Father was heard, the Holy Spirit seen, and the Son baptized.[4] No wonder then that [the Jordan's] very power, which Naaman sensed in his body at the bidding of the prophet,[5] the entire faithful people experience in their soul at the command of Christ.

---

1   2 Kings 5:12.
2   2 Kings 2:8, 14.
3   Josh 3:15; 4:18.
4   Lk 3:22.
5   2 Kings 5:14. See Bernard's sermon for Easter 3; SBOp 5:103-109; CF 52 (forthcoming); and Sentences, Series 3.88; SBOp 6/2:130-135; CF 55:277-284.

# CHAPTER TEN

## MOUNT CALVARY

THEN WE GO OUT TO MOUNT CALVARY[1] where the true Elisha,[2] was jeered by foolish servants[3] and let into his eternal joke his very own children, of whom he says, *Behold, I and my children whom God has given me.*[4] These are good children, by contrast with those malicious ones,[5] children whom the psalmist exhorts to praise, saying, *Praise the Lord, O children, praise the name of the Lord.'*[6]

Praise is enhanced in the mouths of holy infants and sucklings[7] just as it is impaired in the mouths of the envious, those of whom he complains thus: *I have nurtured my children and raised them up, but they have spurned me.'*[8] He ascended the cross, accordingly; our Bald-Pate himself went up,[9] exposed to the world for the sake of the world, with bared head and unveiled face,[10] making atonement for sin.[11] To deliver us from eternal shame[12] and to restore us to glory, he took no shame in the ignominy of a bleak and des-

---

[1]  *Calvariae locum*: the place of the skull. Jn 19:17.

[2]  2 Kings 2:23.

[3]  Mt 27:39; Mk 14:65. Bernard is playing on the double meaning of the Latin *puer* which can mean either boy or servant.

[4]  Is 8:18; Heb 2:13.

[5]  2 Kings 2:23; Ps 21:17.

[6]  Ps 112:1.

[7]  Ps 8:3.

[8]  Is 1:2.

[9]  2 Kings 2:23. A play on *calvus* (bald) and *calvariae locum*.

[10]  2 Cor 3:18.

[11]  Heb 1:3.

[12]  Ps 77:66; Jer 23:40.

picable death nor did he shrink from its torment. No wonder.
What did he have to be ashamed of? He washed us from our
sins,[13] not as water which itself becomes polluted as it cleanses,
but as a sunbeam which dries up filth and itself remains pure.
Indeed he is the very wisdom of God[14] whose purity pen-
etrates everywhere.[15]

---

13  Rev 1:5.
14  1 Cor 1:24.
15  Wis 7:24.

# CHAPTER ELEVEN

## THE HOLY SEPULCHER

O F ALL THE HOLY AND WONDROUS PLACES, somehow the holy Sepulchre hold pride of place. I do not know why people feel a greater devotion at the place where he lay while dead than at the places where he did things while alive,[1] or are more moved by the remembrance of his death than of his life. I suppose that the one is regarded as more desolate, and the other more pleasant; or that the peace of his repose fascinates human weakness more than does the hard toil of his way of life; the security of his death more than the righteousness of his life.

Christ's life has provided a pattern for living for me, but his death, a release from death. The one prepared life, the other destroyed death.[2] His life was arduous but his death was precious; but both are absolutely necessary. What can it be about Christ that is of greater significance: his death to a person living iniquitously or his life to a person dying damnably? Does the death of Christ not deliver from eternal death those who now sin unto death, and did the holiness of his life not deliver the saints who had died before Christ? Is it not written, *What man who is alive will never see death, or can pluck his soul from the grip of hell?*[3]

Now then, since both are equally necessary for us— living faithfully[4] and dying trustingly—by living he taught us how to live and by dying how to die a trusting death. For he died as one des-

---

[1]   Bar 3:38.

[2]   2 Tim 1:10.

[3]   Ps 88:49.

[4]   Tit 2:2.

tined to be raised up again and to those who suffer death brought the hope of rising again. But he has added a third gift as well, without which the other two would count for naught, and that is the remission of sins. For what—insofar as true and supreme happiness is concerned—would goodness, uprightness, or length of life do for anyone still bound by sin, even if only original sin? Death indeed is but the consequence of sin,[5] and if man had avoided sin he would never, ever have tasted death.[6]

19. By sinning then humankind lost life and found death, just as God had forewarned; and it was perfectly just that a person die if he sinned. [7] What could be more just than to bear retaliation?[8] God is indeed the life of the soul, as the soul is the life of the body. By willfully sinning, [the soul] willingly gave up living, and by not choosing life, it also gives up bestowing life. Freely it rejected life since it did not choose to live; it is no longer able to bestow life where and when it pleases. The soul did not want to be governed by God; it is unable to govern its body. How can it command an inferior if it does not submit to its superior? The Creator has found his creature in rebellion against him; the soul will find its lackey a rebel as well. Humankind has been found guilty of transgressing divine law,[9] and he finds another law in his members resisting the rule of his mind and imprisoning him in the law of sin.[10]

Sin indeed, as it is written, separates us from God;[11] and death will separate us from our bodies as well. The soul cannot be separated from God except by sin, nor can the body be separated from the soul except by death. Where is the injustice of its punishment when it is only suffering from its subject the same revolt

---

5    Rom 6:23.

6    Jn 8:51-52.

7    Gen 2:17.

8    Ex 21:23; Deut 19:21: *Lex talionis*, literally, the Law of the Talon.

9    Jas 2:11.

10   Rom 7:23.

11   Is 59:2.

which it contrived against its Creator? Nothing could be more appropriate than that death should have caused death—spiritual death causing one that is physical, a culpable death causing one that is penal, and a willful death one that is constrained.

20. Because therefore humankind was condemned to a twofold death according to our double nature—a voluntary spiritual death and an imposed physical death—the God-Man mercifully and powerfully banished both by his own death, both physical and voluntary. And this one death of his has canceled our double death. This was quite fitting, for of our two deaths, the first we deserved by our fault and the second we owed in punishment. Accepting the punishment, yet without participating in the fault, he underwent a voluntary but only physical death and won for us both life and justice. Otherwise, if he had not suffered physically, he would not have paid what was owed, and if he had not died willingly his death would have been without merit. Now then, if death is what sin deserves and death is what sin owes, as we have seen, then Christ in remitting the sin and dying for sinners has removed both what is deserved and what is owed.

21. How do we know moreover that Christ is able to forgive sins? Doubtless because he is God[12] and can do whatever he wills. But how do we know that he is God? His miracles proved it. He did things which nobody else was able to do[13]—to say nothing of the oracles of the Prophets[14] or the heavenly testimony of the Father's voice coming down to him from majestic glory.[15] If God is for us, who is against us?[16] It is God who justifies, who can condemn?[17] If it is he and no other[18] to whom we daily confess, 'Against you alone have I sinned,'[19] who better, or rather who else, can forgive

---

12 Lk 5:21.
13 Jn 15:24.
14 Is 9:5.
15 2 Pet 1:17; Mt 17:5.
16 Rom 8:31.
17 Rom 8:33-34.
18 Deut 4:35; Is 45:18.
19 Ps 50:6.

what has been committed against him alone? How could he—
who is able to do all things—not be able [to forgive].[20] I can forgive something done to me, if I choose, so can God not also remit
offenses against himself? If then the Almighty, and he alone
against whom we have sinned, can forgive sins,[21] then surely
blessed is he to whom the Lord imputes no sin.[22] Therefore we
recognize that Christ is able to remit sins by the power of
his divinity.

22. And who can doubt that he is willing to do so? He put on
our flesh and endured our death; do you think he will refuse us
his justice? He freely took flesh,[23] freely suffered and was freely
crucified;[24] will he withhold only justice from us? What he is
plainly able to do in virtue of his divinity, he is clearly willing to
do in virtue of his humanity.

But again, how are we confident that he has overcome death?
Precisely because he did not deserve it, but endured it. Why
would anything more be demanded of us in payment which he
has already satisfied in our stead? He who has taken on what our
sin deserved, while bestowing his justice on us, has himself paid
death's debt and restored life. Life will return once death is dead,[25]
just as justice is re-established once sin is removed. Moreover,
death has been put to flight by the death of Christ[26] and the justice of Christ is now counted as our own.

How could he who is God really die? How, except that he was
also man? But by what arrangement could the death of that one
man be credited to another? How, except that this man was just?[27]
Obviously because he was a man, he was able to die; because he

---

20   Wis 7:27; Mt 28:18.
21   Lk 5:21.
22   Ps 31:2.
23   Heb 10:7.
24   Jn 10:18.
25   Hos 13:14.
26   1 Cor 15:54.
27   Lk 23:47.

was a just man, he did not die to no purpose. Of course, one sinner cannot discharge the debt of death for another sinner, since each must die for himself. But why should the death of the one who had no need to die for himself not be of benefit to others? The more undeservedly he died, who did not deserve to die, the more justly will those, for whom he dies, live.

23. 'But what kind of justice is this', you may ask, 'that the innocent should die for the guilty?'[28] It is not justice, but mercy. If it were justice, he would have died, not freely, but deservedly. If deservedly, he would have died indeed, but those for whom he died would not have lived. But if this is not justice, neither is it contrary to justice. Otherwise he could not at the same time be both just and merciful.[29]

'But even if a just man can not unjustly make satisfaction for a sinner, yet by what arrangement can one man satisfy the debts of many? Justice would seem to be stretched quite enough if one life is redeemed by another's death.' This the Apostle has already answered: *Just as all men were condemned by the offense of one man,' he says, so all men receive the justification of life through the justice of one. Just as by the disobedience of one man many were made sinners, so by the obedience of one many will be made just.*[30] 'But perhaps the one who can restore justice to many cannot restore life?' *Death came by one man*, we read, *and by one man came life. As in Adam all have died, so in Christ shall all be made alive.*[31] Then what? One man sins and all persons are considered guilty; shall the innocence of the other be imputed to him alone? The sin of one has caused the death of all; shall the justice of the other restore only one to life? Is the justice of God then more apt to condemn than to pardon? Can Adam do more harm than Christ can good? Shall the sin of Adam be held against me and the justice of Christ not be extended to me? Shall the disobedience of

---

28  1 Pet 3:18; Rom 5:6.
29  2 Mac 1:24.
30  Rom 5:18-19.
31  1 Cor 15:21-22.

the one doom me, and the obedience of the other do nothing for me?

24. 'But,' you will say, 'we have all contracted the guilt of Adam, since we have all participated in his sin.[32] When he sinned we were in him, and we have been begotten from his flesh through the yearnings of the flesh.'[33] Yes, but we are born even more closely related to God by spirit than to Adam by flesh; according to the spirit, we were present in Christ long before we were in Adam according to the flesh. At least we were, if we are convinced that we are counted among those of whom the Apostle says, *He has chosen us in him* (meaning, the Father in the Son) *before the foundation of the world.*'[34] That they are also born of God, the evangelist John attests when he speaks of those, *who are born not of blood, nor of the will of the flesh, nor of the will of man, but of God.*'[35] Again in his letter he says, *Anyone who is born of God does not sin,*[36] because his celestial heritage preserves him.

'But,' you say, 'the presence of the carnal heritage is betrayed by carnal concupiscence, and the sin which we sense in the flesh clearly proves that we are the carnal posterity of the sinner's flesh.' Yet that spiritual begetting is no less sensed, not, of course, in the flesh, but at least in the hearts of those who can say with Paul, We, however, have the sense of Christ.[37] They sense that they have progressed to the point that they can say in total confidence:[38] *The Spirit himself bears witness to our spirit that we are the children of God;*'[39] and again: *We have received, not the spirit of this world, but the Spirit which is of God, that we may recognize the gift*

---

32  Rom 5:12.

33  1 Jn 2:16: *per concupiscentia carnis.*

34  Eph 1:4.

35  Jn 1:13.

36  1 Jn 3:9.

37  1 Cor 2:16: *sensum Christi*, used with the verb *sensit*, translated here a 'experience'.

38  Acts 4:29.

39  Rom 8:16.

*we have received from God.'*[40] By the Spirit which comes from
God, therefore, his love is poured forth into our hearts,[41] just as
by the flesh which comes from Adam, concupiscence remains
embedded in our bodies. As the one coming to us from the flesh
of the first father is never absent from the flesh in this mortal life,
so the other, proceeding from the Father of spirits, never departs[42]
from the wills of his true sons.

25. If we are born of God[43] and chosen in Christ, then what kind
of justice is it that our human and earthly begetting does more
harm than our godly and heavenly does good? That our fleshly
ancestry outweighs God's choice, and flesh passed on temporally
by concupiscence frustrates his eternal design? No, surely, if death
came by one man,[44] why should life not far more readily come by
one, by that very man? If in Adam we have all died, why will we
all not far more potently be brought to life in Christ?[45] Indeed,
*There is no proportion between the gift and the fault.*[46] *Judgment
against one person led to condemnation; yet grace has delivered [us]
from many faults to justification.*[47]

Christ therefore can both forgive sins, because he is God, and die,
because he is a man. In dying [48] he could pay our death dues,
because he is just,[49] and one man could restore all persons to life
and justice, just as sin and death were communicated to every-
one by one [man].

26. But it was also foreseen as utterly necessary that death be
delayed and he live for a while as a man among men, so that by

---

40  1 Cor 2:12.
41  Rom 5:5.
42  1 Cor 13:8.
43  Jn 1:13.
44  Rom 5:12, 17.
45  1 Cor 15:22.
46  Rom 5:15.
47  Rom 5:16.
48  Gen 2:17.
49  Lk 23:47.

his repeated and truth-filled utterances he might stimulate them to desire things invisible, that by his mighty works he might strengthen their faith, and that by his righteous example he might instruct them. Therefore the God-Man lived a sober, righteous, and faithful life in the sight of men;[50] he spoke the truth, worked wonders, and suffered indignities. What then was lacking for our salvation save the grace of the forgiveness of sins? That is, he remitted sins freely; and the work of our salvation was truly then complete.

Have no fear that, as God, he lacked the power to remit sin for sinners or, as the sufferer—suffering so greatly—, the will to do so, provided that we are found to be careful in imitating his example as we should, in venerating his miracles, in believing his teachings, and in being not ungrateful for his sufferings.

27. Everything in Christ therefore benefitted us, everything was highly necessary and highly salutary, his weakness no less than his majesty. Although in demanding it, he removed the yoke of sin by the power of his divinity, yet in dying, he canceled the rights of death by the weakness of his flesh. The Apostle expressed this beautifully when he said: *The weakness of God is stronger than men.'*[51] Yes, and even by his foolishness by which it pleased him to save the world,[52] he confounds the wise in order to refute worldly wisdom.[53] For although he was in the form of God and equal to God he emptied himself, taking the form of a servant.[54] Rich as he was, he became poor for our sakes.[55] Great as he was, he became slight,[56] and elevated as he was, humble.[57] Strong, he became weak, he suffered hunger[58] and thirst,[59] he grew weary in

---

50  Tit 2:12.
51  1 Cor 1:25.
52  1 Cor 1:21.
53  1 Cor 1:27.
54  Phil 2:6-7.
55  2 Cor 8:9.
56  Is 9:6.
57  Mt 11:29.
58  Mt 4:2.
59  Jn 19:28.

his travels,[60] and suffered many other things from choice rather than from necessity. All these were for him a sort of foolishness, but for us were they not the path of prudence,[61] the model of justice, and the paradigm of holiness? This is why the Apostle also said: *The foolishness of God is wiser than men.*'[62]

His death delivered us from death, his life from error, and his grace from sin. Indeed his death was victorious because of his justice, since in repaying what he had not stolen[63] the Just Man acquired a perfect right to reclaim what he had lost. As for his life, it constituted for us by its wisdom a model and mirror of life and knowledge.[64] And his grace indeed, as has been said, forgave sin by that very power which is able to do whatever it wills.[65] Christ's death therefore is the death of my death,[66] because he died that I might live. How could someone for whom Life died fail to be alive? How can anyone still be afraid of going astray in the knowledge of life and reality when Wisdom is his guide? Again, how can anyone be judged guilty whom Justice has absolved? In the Gospel he showed himself to us as Life when he said, I am the Life.[67] As for the two others, we have the testimony of the Apostle who said: *He is become for us Justice and Wisdom unto God the Father.*[68]

28. If then the law of the Spirit of Life has delivered us in Jesus Christ from the law of sin and death,[69] why do we still die, instead of being immediately clothed with immortality?[70] Surely so that the truth of God may be upheld. Because God loves both

---

60  Jn 4:6.

61  Is 40:14.

62  1 Cor 1:25.

63  Ps 68:5.

64  Sir 45:6.

65  Ps 134:6. See above, n. 21.

66  Hos 13:14.

67  Jn 14:6.

68  1 Cor 1:30. Paul did not say 'the Father' but implies it.

69  Rom 8:2.

70  1 Cor 15:53; 2 Cor 5:3.

mercy and truth,[71] it is necessary that man die, as God has foretold;[72] but also that he rise from the dead,[73] lest God forget to be merciful.[74] So, then, although death is not to reign forever, it remains with us for a while now because of God's truth.[75] In the same way sin is not quite absent from us, even though it no longer reigns in our mortal bodies.[76] Similarly, Paul glories on the one hand in being liberated from the law of sin and death,[77] yet on the other he still complains that he is encumbered by some law. He cries out against the law of sin, protesting, *I find another law in my members . . .*[78] and he also groans beneath the burden (doubtless of the law of death) awaiting the redemption of his body.[79]

29. These thoughts and others of this sort regarding the holy sepulcher present themselves to the reflection of Christians according to the attractions of each.[80] I suspect that the tender devotion which floods the person pondering this, while not slight, is not equal to that of someone who sees the Lord's actual resting place with his physical eyes. Even though this place is now empty of its sacred contents, it remains full of delightful mysteries for us. For us, I say, for us, because it is really our resting place. At least it is if we take seriously what we indubitably remember the Apostle saying: *By baptism we are buried together with Christ in death, so that just as Christ rose from the dead to the glory of his Father, so we too may walk in newness of life. If we have been buried together with him in the likeness of his death, we shall also be raised up with him.*[81]

---

71   Ps 83:12; Ps 84:11.

72   Gen 2:17, 3:19.

73   Is 26:19; Mt 16:21.

74   Ps 76:10.

75   Rom 15:8.

76   Rom 6:12.

77   Rom 8:2.

78   Rom 7:23.

79   2 Cor 5:4.

80   Rom 14:5.

81   Rom 6:4-5.

How sweet it must be for pilgrims after the great exhaustion of their long journey, after the many perils of land and sea[82] there at last to find rest  where they know their Lord rested! I should imagine that in their joy they no longer feel the weariness of the journey nor regret the burden of the expense, but, having finished their course[83] and claimed the prize of their labor, as Scripture says, *They rejoice exceedingly to have found the tomb.*[84]

We should not be so foolish as to suppose that the holy sepulcher gained its fame by fluke or chance or by the fickle winds of popularity, when Isaiah so openly and so long ago foretold it, saying: *In that day the root of Jesse will stand as a banner before the peoples, the gentiles shall entreat him and his resting place shall be greatly honored.*[85] Surely, we are now seeing the fulfillment of this prophecy. New to the eye, it is ancient to the ear; as happiness accompanies the novelty, so authority is not absent from antiquity. But enough about the holy sepulcher.

---

82   2 Cor 11:26.
83   1 Cor 9:24.
84   Job 3:22.
85   Is 11:10.

# CHAPTER TWELVE

## BETHPHAGE

WHAT SHALL I SAY OF BETHPHAGE, the village of priests which I almost passed over and which symbolizes both the sacrament of confession and the mystery of priestly ministry? For 'Bethphage' is translated as 'the house of the mouth.'[1] And it is written, The word is near, in your very mouth and in your heart.[2] Remember to keep the word not only in one, but in both at once. In the heart of a sinner the word brings about a salutary contrition, while in the mouth it relieves a noxious confusion which may inhibit necessary confession.

As Scripture says, There is a shame leading to sin, and there is also a shame leading to glory.[3] The good shame leads you to blush at having sinned or certainly at sinning. Even though not a single human witness is present, you will be more disconcerted by divine than by human scrutiny, given that God's purity is so much greater than man's, and that, in proportion to his greater distance from all sin, he is more offended by the sinner. Shame of this sort avoids reproach and prepares for glory, for it either eliminates sin entirely, or at least punishes it by penance and removes it by confession, if only this is our boast, the testimony of a good conscience.

But if anyone is ashamed to confess the cause of his distress, this sort of shame leads to sin and forfeits the glory of a good con-

---

1    That is, the mouth or entrance of the valley, according to Jerome. Others read 'house of green figs'. And many other interpretations are given. See Jerome, *Liber de nominibus hebraicis*, PL 23:839-840.

2    Deut 30:14; Rom 10:8.

3    Sir 4:25.

science.[4] The evil which compunction spurs him to cast from his heart is now unable to pass the lips which have been sealed by this misplaced shame. He ought instead to follow the example of David and say, *I have not sealed my lips*, O Lord, you know it.[5]

David, I think, was reproaching himself for this sort of absurd and unreasonable shame when he said, Because I was silent, my bones grew old.[6] That is why he hoped that a gate might be placed before his lips, so that the portal of his mouth might be open to confession, but closed to excuses.[7] In fact, he quite plainly requested this of the Lord in prayer, knowing all too well that confession and magnificence are his works.[8] We should not remain silent concerning the magnificence of his divine goodness and power, nor hide our own malice. This double confession is a great good, but it is also a gift of God.[9] Therefore he prays, *Do not incline my heart to evil words, or to making excuses for my sins.*[10]

This is why priests, as ministers of the Word, must remain carefully solicitous toward erring hearts, using such moderation in the administering of the word of contrition and fear as will not frighten them away from the word of confession. They should open hearts in a way that does not close mouths. But they should not absolve even the contrite unless they see them also making confession; since indeed, one believes in the heart and is justified; but one confess with the mouth and is saved.[11] On the other hand, confession is lost to the dead as if they did not exist.[12] Anyone therefore who has the word in his mouth but not in his heart is either deceitful or vain, while someone who has it in his heart but not in his mouth is either proud or craven.

---

4    Sir 4:25.
5    Ps 39:10.
6    Ps 31:3.
7    Ps 140:3-4.
8    Ps 110:3.
9    Eph 2:8.
10    Ps 140:4.
11    Rom 10:10.
12    Sir 17:26.

# CHAPTER THIRTEEN

## BETHANY

**P**RESSED AS I AM, I ought not to pass over in silence Bethany, the house of obedience[1] This is the village of Mary and Martha, where Lazarus was raised to life.[2] Here, of course, we have held up to us the image of the two ways of life, and of God's wonderful mercy towards sinners,[3] as well as of the virtue of obedience—one with the fruits of penance.

Here[4] we need only briefly indicate that neither zeal for good works[5] nor the repose of holy contemplation[6] nor the tears of penance[7] are acceptable to him except in 'Bethany;' for he so prized obedience that he chose it over life, being made obedient to his Father even unto death.[8]

These surely are those riches promised in prophecy by the word of the Lord: *The Lord will console Sion, he says, he will strengthen all her ruins, and take his delight in her wastes. He will make her deserts as the garden of the Lord. Gladness and rejoicing will be found in her, the voice of praise and thanksgiving.*[9] These delights of

---

1     Bernard again follows Jerome here, *Liber de nominibus hebraicis*, PL 23:849-40. Others have 'house of the poor', and many other derivations.

2     Jn 11:1.

3     Jn 11:38-44. Lazarus' four days in the tomb is understood as a figure of the soul in sin.

4     Bernard develops this theme at length in his sermons on the Assumption. See especially, Asspt 3; SBOp 5:238-244.

5     Of which Martha is the type; see Lk 10:40-41.

6     Of which Mary is the type; see Lk 10:39, 42.

7     Of which Lazarus is the type; see Jn 11:31.

8     Phil 2:8.

9     Is 51:3.

the world, this heavenly treasure and this heritage of all faithful people is now entrusted to your care, beloved brothers, commended to your prudence and your courage. Yet you will be able to keep this heavenly trust safely and faithfully only if you rely, not on your own prudence and courage, but on God's help, knowing that no man prevails by his own strength,[10] and therefore repeating with the prophet, *The Lord is my support, my refuge and my liberator,*[11] and again, *To you do I look for my strength, O God, my protector; my God whose mercy goes before me.*[12] Always say, *Not unto us O Lord, not unto us, but unto your own name, give the glory,*[13] so that in all things he may be blessed who teaches your hands to war and your fingers to fight.[14]

---

10  1 Sam 2:9.

11  Ps 17:3.

12  Ps 58:10-11.

13  Ps 113:9. (Ps 113b:1).

14  Ps 143:1.

# SELECTED BIBLIOGRAPHY

## CRITICAL EDITION

'Liber ad Milites Templi: de laude novae militiae.' Ed. J. Leclercq and H. M. Rochais. *S. Bernardi Opera*. Vol. 3. Rome: Editiones Cistercienses, 1963: 312-239.

## TRANSLATIONS

Charpentier, M. 'Louange de la nouvelle milice des templiers,' *Oeuvres complètes de saint Bernard*. Vol. 2. Paris: Vives, 1866. 388-412.

De Solms, E. 'A la louange de la milice nouvelle,' *Saint Bernard*. Namur: Soleil Levant, 1958: 152-191.

Diez Ramos, G. 'De la excelencia de la Nueva Milicia,' *Obras completas de San Bernardo*. Vol. 2, Biblioteca de Autores Cristianos 130. Madrid: Editorial Catolica, 1955: 853-881.

## STUDIES

Barber, Malcolm. *The New Knighthood. A History of the Order of the Temple*. Cambridge 1994.

Bulst-Thiele, M.-L. 'The Influence of St. Bernard of Clairvaux on the Formation of the Knights Templar', in M. Gervers, ed. *The Second Crusade and the Cistercians*. New York 1992. Pp. 57-65.

Carlson, D. 'The Practical Theology of Saint Bernard and the Date of the *De laude novae militiae*', in John R. Sommerfeldt, ed., *Studies in Medieval Cistercian History* 11 (Kalamazoo 1987) 133-147.

Carrière, V. 'Les débuts de l'Ordre du Temple en France,' *Le Moyen Age*, 18 (1914) 308-334.

*Cartulaire général de l'Ordre du Temple.* Ed. Marquis d'Albon. 2 vols. Paris, 1913. Note especially, *Regula commilitonum Christi*, ed. G. Schnürer, 1:129-153.

Charrier, H. 'Les sens militaire chez saint Bernard,' *Saint Bernard et son temps.* 2 vols. Dijon, 1929: 1:68-74.

Commission d'Histoire de l'Ordre de Cîteaux. *Bernard de Clairvaux.* Paris: Alsatia, 1953. See especially the *Table analytique* V, 6, pp. 673-674.

Cousin, P. 'Les débuts de l'Ordre des Templiers et saint Bernard,' *Mélanges saint Bernard.* Dijon: Trouve, 1953: 41-52.

De Curzon, H., ed. *La Règle du Temple.* Paris, 1886.

Delaruelle, E. 'L'Idée de croisade chez saint Bernard,' *Mélanges saint Bernard*: pp. 53-67.

De Poorter, A. 'Le texte original de la Règle des Templiers,' *Annual de la Societé d'Emulation de Bruges*, 62 (1912) 193-198.

Dessubré, M. *Bibligraphie de l'ordre des Templiers.* Paris, 1928.

Elm, Kaspar. *Umbilicus Mundi. Beiträge zur Geschichte Jerusalems, der Kreuzzüge, des Kapitels vom Heiligen Grab in Jerusalem unter der Ritterorden.* Instrumenta Canonissarum Regularium Sancti Sepulcri 6. Sint-Kruis: Sint-Tudo=Abdij 1998.

Hugh [of Payens (?)]. *Epistola.* Ed. Jean Leclercq. *Recueil d'études sur saint Bernard et ses écrits.* Vol. 2. Rome, 1966: 93-96.

Leclercq, Jean. 'Un document sur les débuts des Templiers.' *Renue d'histoire ecclésiastique* 52 (1957) 81-91. Recueil 2: 87-100.

Léonard, M. *Introduction au Cartulaire manuscrit del'Ordre du Temple.* Paris, 1930.

Lobet, M. *L'histoire mystérieuse et tragique des Templiers.* Liège, 1944.

Luddy, Ailbe J. *Life and Teaching of Saint Bernard.* Dublin: Gill, 1950. See especially, pp. 172-178.

Luttrell, A. 'The Earliest Templars', in M. Balard, ed. *Autour de la Première Croisade.* Paris 1996. PP. 193-202.

Melville, M. *La vie des Templiers.* Paris: Gallimard, 1951.

Oliver, A. 'El Libre del Ordre de Cavalleria' de Ramon Llull y et 'De laude Novae Militia' de s. Bernard,' *Estudios Llulianos,* 8 (1958) 175-186.

Pensoye, P. 'Saint Bernard et la règle du Temple.' *Études Traditionelles,* 364 (1961) 81-88.

Prawer, Joshua. *Histoire du royaume latin de Jérusalem.* Paris, 1969.

Rousset, P. 'Les origines et la caractère de la Deuzième Croisade, Saint Bernard et la Croisade,' *Saint Bernard et son temps.* 1:152-168.

Schnürer, G. *Die Ursprüngliche Templerregel.* Freiburg-im-Breisgau, 1903.

_____. 'Zur ersten Organization der Templer,' *Historisches Jahrbuch,* 32 (1911) 298-314.

Sclafert, C. 'Lettre inédite de Hugues de Saint-Victor aux Chevaliers du Temple,' *Revue d'ascétique et de mystique* 34 (1958) 276-299.

Selwood, D. '*Quidam autem dubitaverunt*: The Saint and the Sinner, the Temple and a Possible Chronology,' in M. Balard, ed., *Autour de la Première Croisade,* Paris 1996.

Seward, Desmond. 'Dissolution of the Templars,' *History Today,* 31 (1971) 628- 635.

William of Tyr. *Historia rerum transmarinarum,* Liber 21, c. 7; PL 201:526-527.

Williams, E. 'Cîteaux et la seconde croisade.' *Revue d'histoire ecclésiastique,* 49 (1954) 116-151.

# INDEX TO
# IN PRAISE OF THE NEW KNIGHTHOOD

# SCRIPTURAL INDEX

| | | | | |
|---|---|---|---|---|
| Jn 10:14 | 60 | | Rom 10:8 | 77 |
| Jn 10:18 | 68 | | Rom 10:10 | 78 |
| Jn 11:1 | 79 | | Rom 12:10 | 46 |
| Jn 11:31 | 79 | | Rom 13:4 | 39 |
| Jn 11:38-44 | 79 | | Rom 14:5 | 74 |
| Jn 12:31 | 60 | | Rom 14:8 | 34 |
| Jn 13:18 | 60 | | Rom 15:8 | 74 |
| Jn 14:6 | 73 | | | |
| Jn 15:24 | 67 | | 1 Cor 1:21 | 72 |
| Jn 18:12 | 56 | | 1 Cor 1:24 | 64 |
| Jn 19:1 | 56 | | 1 Cor 1:25 | 72, 73 |
| Jn 19:17 | 63 | | 1 Cor 1:27 | 72 |
| Jn 19:28 | 72 | | 1 Cor 1:30 | 73 |
| Jn 20:29 | 54 | | 1 Cor 2:2 | 54 |
| | | | 1 Cor 2:6 | 54 |
| Acts 4:29 | 70 | | 1 Cor 2:8 | 56 |
| Acts 4:32 | 46 | | 1 Cor 2:12 | 71 |
| Acts 9:1-22 | 51 | | 1 Cor 2:13 | 54 |
| | | | 1 Cor 2:15 | 60 |
| Rom 2:11 | 46 | | 1 Cor 2:16 | 70 |
| Rom 3:38 | 34 | | 1 Cor 3:2 | 54 |
| Rom 5:5 | 71 | | 1 Cor 9:10 | 37 |
| Rom 5:6 | 69 | | 1 Cor 9:24 | 75 |
| Rom 5:12 | 70 | | 1 Cor 11:14 | 47 |
| Rom 5:12, 17 | 71 | | 1 Cor 11:31 | 59 |
| Rom 5:15 | 71 | | 1 Cor 13:8 | 71 |
| Rom 5:16 | 71 | | 1 Cor 15:21-22 | 69, 71 |
| Rom 5:18-19 | 69 | | 1 Cor 15:53 | 73 |
| Rom 6:4-5 | 74 | | 1 Cor 15:54 | 68 |
| Rom 6:12 | 74 | | | |
| Rom 6:23 | 66 | | 2 Cor 3:15 | 56 |
| Rom 7:23 | 66, 74 | | 2 Cor 3:18 | 63 |
| Rom 8:2 | 73, 74 | | 2 Cor 5:3 | 73 |
| Rom 8:3 | 56 | | 2 Cor 5:4 | 74 |
| Rom 8:16 | 70 | | 2 Cor 5:16 | 53 |
| Rom 8:31 | 67 | | 2 Cor 8:9 | 72 |
| Rom 8:33-34 | 67 | | 2 Cor 10:4-5 | 41 |

### Index of Citations of the Rule

Lightning Source UK Ltd.
Milton Keynes UK
UKHW040647140421
381968UK00001B/26

9 780879 071202